Heart of the

THE RESURRECTION
Volume II

Gary R. Habermas

COLLEGE PRESS
PUBLISHING COMPANY
Joplin, Missouri

International Standard Book Number 0-89900-843-7

CONTENTS

Series Introduction 5

Study Introduction 7

1 Transformed Lives and the
     Birth of the Church 12

2 Evangelism 29

3 Christian Doubt 45

4 Grief, Suffering, and Pain 67

5 Daily Power and Praise 86

6 The Christian Ethics of Total Commitment 108

7 Fear of Death 122

Conclusion: The Center of
     New Testament Practice 142

2000 AND BEYOND
STUDIES FOR SMALL GROUPS

In pursuit of our stated goal, "Every Christian a Bible Student," College Press has, since 1995, been publishing a series of *Studies for Small Groups*. These have proved very popular, both for group and individual study on a variety of topics and Scripture texts. Although, with the year 2000, we have changed the outward appearance of these study booklets, our commitment is still to providing solid, thought-provoking studies that will make a life-changing difference in the reader.

Of course, although we call these studies "for small groups," they are equally suited for individual study. If you are simply reading the book for your own benefit, please do take the time to use the "Reflecting on . . ." questions to focus your own thoughts. In a small group study, the questions should not only be used as a review, to see if you remember what was actually said in that lesson by the writer, but to help spark discussion of the further *implications* of the lesson material. Nor should you consider the questions that are provided the only questions to be asked. Any study is only as good as the effort you put into it, and the group leader should have read the lesson through thoroughly before the class meets, as well as encouraging all other members of the group to do so if possible. If the leader has gone through the lesson in advance, he or she will probably have thought of other questions, some of which may never have even occurred to the writer or editors of the study. After all, what is important is not just the bare facts of the lesson, but how they intersect with your own path in the Christian walk.

Above all, do not feel you have to race through the lessons. Although the number of lessons is purposely kept small so that no one has to commit in advance to an endless period of time on the study, you should not cut off discussion of an important issue just to fit the whole of the lesson into one study session. Nor do you want to leave off the end of a lesson because you didn't get it all in during the allotted time. The greatest advantage of the small group setting is the flexibility you have, allowing you to carry over discussion to the next session. Take full advantage of this flexibility.

THE RESURRECTION: HEART OF THE CHRISTIAN LIFE

At our family reunions, there is a joke that gets told and retold every time we're all together. We never get tired of it. It takes several forms, but the theme is always the same. I'm the one with the library; I teach and write books, but I can't really DO anything else. My brother Kevin doesn't like books or public speaking, but he's the DOER. He fixes or builds anything. I own books — he owns tools.

So when we're all visiting together and something needs to be fixed, someone will call out: "Go borrow Gary's tools. He's got plenty."

"Yeah, someone else counters — if you want little kiddie toys that don't really work anyway." Everyone enjoys the laugh, including me.

But I suspect that a very similar message is popular regarding subjects like philosophy, theology, and apologetics. It is widely believed among Christians that here we are dealing only with theory, very seldom touching the "real" world of evangelism, junior church, and hurting people. The theoretical "thinkers" are those who wade into the pithiest issues where angels fear to tread and are frequently ready for any debate. They are separated from the pragmatic "doers" — those who know how to build churches, keep the youth interested, lead worship, and minister to those who seek help.

Can the two sides ever meet somewhere in the middle? Can the doers' ministries be strengthened by a strong dose of theory? Could this actually, somehow, increase the effectiveness of their work? Might those who are already so very good at ministry actually gain depth by getting and giving answers that are more specific and more accurate? Could this make their practice even better? Would hurting people receive the help they need?

On the other hand, can the thinkers ever get out and DO something in ministry? While we certainly need more depth, especially among evangelicals who often come out a bit short in this department, is there ever a time to put our questions on the shelf, at least briefly, and try to apply our answers? For example, while we may know the best solution to the perennial problems of pain and evil, do we really know if these responses work in the real world with hurting people?

This little book is written for those who are interested in the subject of Jesus' resurrection but who think that it has to be applied where it is needed the most — to ministry situations involving Christians who want to know what the central truth in the New Testament has to say about actually changing lives. For this sort of reader, the fact of the resurrection is crucial, but without all the proofs, arguments, rejoinders, and surrejoinders. Their world is busy enough just being there to plan and support a youth rally, participate in evangelism, or visit the hospital.

Can we pull it off? Can we combine good theory with real application? Can we build bridges between theory and practice? In short, can the truth of the resurrection be brought to bear in the real world? Both sides are necessary. After all, it took both researchers to discover penicillin and nurses to dispense it. Our goal is to make some modest inroads that can really make a difference — in the head as well as in the heart.

This is the second volume in a set. Neither is theoretical. Both are popular and, I hope, practical. To encourage more relevancy and practicality, each chapter in the two volumes contains "Application" and "Reflecting" sections for careful consideration of lessons that can be both learned and applied. Each of these sections, in particular, is devoted to specific suggestions that encourage change. "Suggested Readings" lists are also included with each chapter, composed of general sources of a basic nature. They may be consulted for additional study.

The theme of the first book is that the resurrection of Jesus is not only the central event in the gospel and in the study of apologetics, but in Christian theology as a whole. We explore some of these connections, being careful to note in each chapter several areas of application.

The theme here is that Jesus' resurrection is also the center of our Christian practice. We will link this event to some of the most important areas of the Christian life, also seeking to drive home each lesson with some very specific suggestions for application to some very tough areas where believers are called upon to act.

OUR TOPICS

Lives were clearly changed when people came into contact with the risen Jesus. This not only applied to strong believers, but also to unbelievers like James, the brother of Jesus, and Saul of Tarsus. We will examine what happened to these individuals, as well as taking a look at the church that God used them to start.

Early Christian efforts at evangelism not only centered on the proclamation of Jesus' death and resurrection, but they were inspired by the commands of the risen Jesus Himself. Although there were different methodological emphases in the earliest preaching, both Jews and Gentiles clearly heard the same message.

The topic of Jesus' resurrection is also interwoven throughout the New Testament with living various aspects of the Christian life. It is given the job of going up against the really big problems in life, too. The resurrection is used to encourage doubting believers, as well as those suffering grief because they have already lost a loved one to death. It even comforted those who were undergoing pain and suffering of various other sorts, including persecution for their faith.

Further, the resurrection also provided daily power to Christians for the purpose of overcoming sin and living the Christian life. Praise and worship were directed to the risen Jesus. This event is also the chief reason that we should be totally committed to God.

Finally, the resurrection of Jesus is used in the New Testament to address the believer's fear of death. If this anxiety is the greatest of all, as many would tell us, then we will really get a chance to see if the truth of this event can be applied in some of the toughest circumstances of life.

In a sense, this book is all about integration – about bringing resurrection truth to bear in our daily lives. Perhaps the single theme throughout is that real facts are related to real spirituality. I'm totally convinced that the resurrection of Jesus is the most crucial bridge between reality and life. Knowing the truth of this event is the engine that drives the quest for spiritual victory. The resurrection leads us to the exercise of Christian discipline. Each chapter is an attempt to develop specific practices that encourage Christian living precisely in those areas where believers frequently struggle. God changes the lives of those who practice His truth. The result is a closer relationship with Him, including experiencing His peace.

Our subjects are those where the rubber really meets the road. Scripture is bold enough to say not only that Jesus' resurrection is true, but that, at the same time, it is effective in dealing with life in the trenches. Can it really be that good? Can it assist us in our ministries, providing the motivation we must have in order to reach others? Is it really a balm ready-made for hurting people? Are there really some specific things we can think and practice in order to both gain victories and live above the daily grind? This is what we plan to investigate.

1

TRANSFORMED LIVES
AND THE BIRTH OF THE CHURCH

In this lesson:

> ▶ Cults and commitment
> ▶ The cause of Jesus' disciples' transformation
> ▶ The birth of the church
> ▶ Specific examples of changed lives

The news regularly reports the phenomenon. Another religious cult has been born. Too often, it seems they get publicity for the wrong reasons — building up arms and making threats, planting bombs, plotting somebody's overthrow or other radical political action, believing in some sort of UFO redemption, or having a founder who claims to be the messiah or some special prophet. Several times in recent memory the result was that a number of people died. Sometimes a bloody massacre occurred. On other occasions, it was just a possibility. Perhaps an instance has come to your mind, but actually there are too many examples here to even count. And then, someone compares the cultists to New Testament Christians, as if all theological beliefs and religious transformations were basically the same.

It cannot be denied that many of these cultists are sincere. Some of them have chosen to die for their faith. When that happens, even though the majority of people seem to think that they died in vain, most are generally willing to grant at least two things: the cultists were brave, and they really believed what they said they did.

> It cannot be denied that many cultists are sincere.

Did you ever wonder what it takes to be transformed by some message — even a message that's clearly false? It's pretty clear that someone is wrong when cultists sell all their possessions and await some catastrophic prediction that never occurs. What motivated them to do this? When there is a loss of life, this is particularly distressing. I think that the most crucial matter here is the **person's beliefs**. This is what determines the degree of commitment.

So then, is there really any difference between some of these typical cultists and Christians? How can we make a major distinction on the grounds of belief alone? We believe the teachings of Jesus, and they believe someone else's. What's the distinction here?

WHAT MADE THE DIFFERENCE?

The chief answer to these questions comes from the part played by Jesus' resurrection. In our first volume, *The Resurrection:*

Heart of New Testament Doctrine, we pointed out that this event was central to the New Testament proclamation. It was the chief sign given to unbelievers and believers alike. It indicated that Jesus' teachings were truthful and that salvation was offered to those who trusted the Jesus of the gospel. There were plenty of reasons to believe that the resurrection occurred, too. In fact, Luke the medical doctor and historical researcher chooses Greek words (*en pollios tekmeriois*) that indicate the highest level of evidence for this event (Acts 1:3).

The resurrection indicated that Jesus' teachings were truthful and that salvation was offered to those who trusted the Jesus of the gospel.

Therefore, when we ask why Jesus' disciples were transformed and how their beliefs were different from those of religious cultists, we have to look at the resurrection. This is because it was the foundation of their faith. And this is the chief difference, too. The apostles did not merely believe someone else's claims to be someone special. They made a much more common — and measurable — assertion. They had really seen somebody — the risen Jesus.

Think about it for a minute. Yes, Jesus made extraordinary claims for Himself. In fact, He said things that no other major religious founder ever said.[1] Beyond this, He was seen by His followers after His death just like you would see a friend who had stopped by your home for a visit. Obviously, the resurrection was not a mundane event. But once the miracle occurred, seeing Jesus alive was precisely like meeting a friend. Jesus walked with them, ate the same food they did, and spent hours just talking with them.

So why were the disciples transformed? They had seen Him alive after His death! It made all the difference in the world! They knew that His teachings were true after all! This is what transformed them and what makes Christianity different from all the religions and cults of the world. They knew they had just seen the risen Jesus!

Orthodox followers of the other major world religions do not believe that their founders were raised from the dead. So they are left with a message by itself. True, they were still transformed, but not because there was a miraculous event like the resurrection that confirmed their founder's message. They just decided to believe what they were taught.

But there is another factor that also needs to be mentioned briefly. It is possible that not even all transformations are created equal. Studies have

> Orthodox followers of the other major world religions do not believe that their founders were raised from the dead.

estimated that a high percentage of certain cult converts (perhaps as high as 90%!) defect.[2] It is true that some religious believers in every faith will appear to have given up their belief. But this is an amazingly elevated figure for certain cultists. Perhaps some people are transformed, but only for a brief time. If this figure is true, it just seems that many more forget their beliefs in the cults. This deserves further study.

At any rate, the apostles and others went out to the world armed with the unique messages of Jesus' teaching *and* His resurrection from the dead. There is good evidence that many of them died for their faith,[3] but there are no indications that a single one of them ever recanted. Led by the Holy Spirit, their newly redirected lives were instrumental in the founding of the church. These were unique transformations, based on unique events.

In this chapter we will explore the relationship between Jesus' resurrection and the birth of the Christian church. Then we will look at three separate individuals who were each drastically altered by Jesus' appearances. Our overall purpose will be to show how the earliest Christians were completely transformed by their time with the risen Jesus.

THE BIRTH OF THE CHURCH

In the Gospel accounts of Jesus' resurrection appearances, we are told that He was raised and made His initial appearances on the first day of the week.[4] Another appearance took place the following Sunday (John 20:26). Later we are told that the first day of the week was the regular meeting day for the church.[5] A second-century Christian writing explains that this day signified Jesus' resurrection from the dead (*The Epistle of Barnabas* 15).

The traditional date for the beginning of the Christian church is the Day of Pentecost and the coming of the indwelling Holy Spirit. But we certainly have a precursor in these initial resurrection appearances when Jesus met with His followers on at least two consecutive Sundays.

In another pre-Pentecost meeting, Peter and the other ten apostles decided to seek the Lord's will in choosing a replacement for Judas. The major prerequisite was that the person had been with them from the time John baptized Jesus until the present. In particular, this individual had to be a witness of Jesus' resurrection, again showing the centrality of this event. Two men were suggested and Matthias was chosen to serve as the twelfth apostle (Acts 1:15-26).

After the resurrection appearances of Jesus, His ascension, and the choosing of Matthias, the early believers were gathered together in Jerusalem because of the command of the risen Jesus (Acts 1:4-5,12-14). Then on the Day of Pentecost the Holy Spirit came as Jesus had promised and the church was born (Acts 2:1-4).

> So the resurrection was the event upon which the church was founded.

So the resurrection was the event upon which the church was founded, figuring in at each stage. Jesus' Sunday meetings with His disciples, His command to wait for the coming of the Holy Spirit, and the choosing of Matthias served as precursors. The first two resulted from Jesus' resurrection appearances, while the last was based on them. Indeed, there would be no church apart from Jesus' resurrection. The disciples probably would have returned to their homes and the movement would never have started.

Peter acknowledged this same point in his famous Pentecost sermon by stating that the resurrected Jesus was afterwards exalted to heaven, sending the Holy Spirit to His followers. This was the cause of what happened that day (Acts 2:32-33; cf. John 16:7). The birth of the church was due to the activity of the resurrected Jesus.

As a result of Peter's initial message on the Day of Pentecost, at least 3,000 persons became believers, were baptized, and were added to the ranks of the church (Acts 2:41). These earliest Christians (as they were later called) were taught by the apostles and fellowshiped together, participating in the Lord's supper and prayer. They practiced a radical form of sharing their material possessions and witnessed miracles done by the apostles. Others were apparently affected, because we are told that new members joined them on a daily basis (Acts 2:42-47). About two thousand more joined their numbers a little later (Acts 4:4). Surprisingly, even a large number of Jewish priests believed (Acts 6:7)!

So Pentecost was the date for the founding of the church but it was only the beginning of apostolic efforts to preach the gospel. As we will see in the next chapter, the death and resurrection of Jesus Christ was the absolute center of their early teaching. This is what had changed them from disillusioned disciples who scattered just prior to Jesus' death into transformed individuals who were willing to die for this message. In purely psychological terms, for such a band of defeated men to have unanimously devoted their lives (sometimes to the death) for this cause with no recorded cases of regret is incredibly amazing. But this is what actually experiencing the message of the gospel did for them — it changed and redirected their views, personalities, occupations, and goals in life. We will showcase this total transformation by highlighting three individual lives.

> The death and resurrection of Jesus Christ was the absolute center of the apostles' early teaching.

THE CASE OF PETER

Probably the best known of the apostles, Peter is sometimes remembered for being the outspoken leader of this group. He often appears to be brash and impetuous — the one most likely to speak up on behalf of the others (see Matt. 16:13-23). Sometimes his insights were of God and he was commended (v. 17). But then, just as quickly, Jesus also rebuked him for his words (vv. 21-23). Yet, Peter was destined to greatness for the Kingdom's sake.

This outspoken, strong leader is perhaps most remembered for his repeated denial of his Lord after first abandoning Him in the garden. No analysis can do justice to the grief Peter felt when, after the denials, he momentarily locked eyes with Jesus, afterwards weeping bitterly (see Luke 22:54-62). His self-incrimination and sense of despair would be terribly difficult to imagine.

However, just a short time later, we find a much more powerful and focused individual preaching the truths of the gospel message without any thought for his own safety. He even boldly proclaimed the death and resurrection in the face of those who might have taken his life. Some of those to whom he spoke may even have called for Jesus' crucifixion. That did not even deter him. But even after imprisonment, a beating, and further threatening, he stood firm. Peter's personality dominates the first 12 chapters of Acts.[6]

How do we explain the profound change in this man? Peter had been an unpredictable individual who once boasted that he would never forsake Jesus even if it meant dying with Him (Matt. 26:35), but then he both abandoned Him and denied Him repeatedly. What

> Without doubt, the event that turned Peter's life around was the resurrection of Jesus.

could possibly account for Peter's transformation into the one who was later quite willing to face death for the sake of the gospel message? He even rejoiced that he was worthy to suffer for Christ (Acts 5:41)! The Jewish leaders were amazed at his courage (Acts 4:13).

We can narrow the time of Peter's change to a fairly specific interval. Whatever accounts for his transformation must have occurred after his denials of the Lord but before his Pentecost sermon about 50 days later. Without doubt, the event that turned his life around was the resurrection of Jesus. Mark tells us that the angels at the empty tomb had a special message for Peter, singling him out for the proclamation that Jesus was risen (16:6-7). Could this have been to reassure him after the despair of his denials? Peter responded by being one of two disciples to run to the empty tomb to check it out for himself (John 20:3-9; cf. Luke 24:12). Further, Peter was apparently the first apostle to see Jesus alive (Luke 24:34; cf. 1 Cor. 15:5). Afterwards, every one of his early speeches was based on the resurrection, ringing out with its truth.[7]

What would it have been like to have witnessed that initial and apparently private meeting between the risen Jesus and the apostle Peter? What words passed between them? What assurance did Peter find this time when he gazed into the depths of Jesus' eyes? No doubt it was a very different sort of look than when he saw Jesus on the night he betrayed Him! I can imagine several hearty hugs and many tears of joy, unlike the bitter tears the night before the crucifixion. We can be sure of two things: Peter must have been totally persuaded that his denials were forgiven, as well as being even more firmly convinced that he had seen Jesus alive. That meeting and others with his resurrected Lord completely transformed his life!

THE CASE OF JAMES

Comparatively less is known about James, the brother of Jesus. Especially given his rather prominent role in the New Testament, relatively little is said about him in the Gospels. We are told that Jesus had brothers (Matt. 12:46-50) and James is mentioned by name as the son of Mary.[8] Interestingly, even the Jewish historian Josephus refers to James as Jesus' brother, noting that Jesus was called the Christ (*Antiquities* 20:9).

But James was also known as an unbeliever — he did not believe the truth of Jesus' message and even taunted Him (John 7:3-5; cf. Matt. 13:54-57). This must have been an odd case of skepticism — a family member who spent part of his life in close proximity to Jesus but who rejected His message. Modern skeptics should understand and appreciate James's stance.

But in the early church, James was a key leader. He is singled out because of his prominent position (Acts 12:17; 21:18).[9] When Paul traveled to Jerusalem shortly after his conversion, he met with Peter and James, to whom he refers as the brother of the Lord (Gal. 1:19).

> Modern skeptics should understand and appreciate James's stance.

Fourteen years later, Paul returned to Jerusalem and met with James, Peter, and John (Gal. 2:1-10). At the Jerusalem Council, where dignitaries such as Peter, Paul, and Barnabas were present, it was James who rendered the final decision (Acts 15:13-21).[10]

Admittedly, this is a startling contrast. At least Peter was already a follower of Jesus. James, on the other hand, changed from an unbeliever to a prominent leader in the early church. But none of the passages above note any reason for his conversion.

However, Paul's text in 1 Corinthians 15:7 provides the needed enlightenment. There we are told that, like Peter, the risen Jesus made a personal appearance to James, too. This must have been another joyous reunion! Details are not provided, but it is not difficult to imagine that emotional meeting where James realized that the older brother he had played with as a child, and later rejected, was the very Son of God, resurrected from the dead! What a shock that must have been! Like Joseph of old, the estranged brothers had been united! This is the only clue we have concerning the reason for James's dramatic change from a skeptic to one of the leaders in the early church.

THE CASE OF PAUL

In spite of the exciting contrasts involved in our first two individuals, it is likely that no personal transformation in the early church was as dramatic as that of Saul of Tarsus, later to become the apostle Paul. A famous persecutor of Christians, Paul approved of Stephen's death (Acts 7:58) and hunted down believers wherever they were (8:1-3). We are told that he "began to destroy the church" (8:3).

> A famous persecutor of Christians, Paul approved of Stephen' s death and hunted down believers wherever they were.

In his own words, Paul described himself as being convinced that he had to do all he could against Christians, imprisoning men and women, trying to get them to blaspheme God, and even being involved in some of their deaths (Acts 22:4-5; 26:9-11). Paul describes his former temperament as an "obsession" against believers, which took him to other cities in his desire to track them down (Acts 26:11).

In addition to his practice of persecuting Christians, Paul described himself as a Pharisee, "a Hebrew of Hebrews" who was spotless regarding the observance of the Old Testament Law. Further, he had studied under the famous Jewish scholar Gamaliel, who had a reputation for being the leading expert on questions pertaining to the Law.[11] Paul even challenged a number of Jews by claiming that he was as zealous as any of his own countrymen.[12]

This same Saul of Tarsus, the Pharisee and scholar who had the best theological training available, now desired to imprison and kill any Christians he could find. It was this combination of scholar-persecutor that makes Paul such an intriguing character as an opponent of Christianity. He combined his scholarship with a zealous hatred of the Christian gospel.

There is no secret about what happened to change Saul of Tarsus into the Apostle Paul, perhaps the greatest Christian theologian and missionary ever. In three extended accounts and a few other brief comments, Paul explains how, in an ultimate confrontation, this scholar-persecutor met the risen Jesus in an episode that forever changed both his life and the Mediterranean world as well.

> There is no secret about what happened to change Saul of Tarsus into the Apostle Paul.

On his way to Damascus to persecute the believers there, Saul and his companions were suddenly struck down by a light described as being brighter than the noontime sun. How did Saul react? He didn't debate or defend himself by arguing passages from the Old Testament or begin making accusations against Christians. Rather, he met and committed his entire life to the risen and glorified Jesus, who commissioned him to preach the gospel to the Gentiles.

The men who were with him heard the voice and witnessed the light. Like him, they also fell to the ground, but in contrast to Saul, they saw no one. Neither did they understand the message given to him.[13] As a result, Saul was blinded for three days (Acts 9:1-9; 22:6-11; 26:12-18).

It is not surprising to find that many Christians were not immediately sure about Saul, perhaps thinking that he was faking conversion in order to infiltrate their ranks. In Damascus, when the Lord told Ananias to go and heal the newly repentant Saul, he reminded the Lord of Paul's persecutions, as if to warn God that they had better be careful (Acts 9:11-16)! When Saul began preaching in Damascus, his listeners were astonished, recalling his previous actions (9:21). In Jerusalem, he tried to join the other believers, but they were afraid of him, doubting that he was truly a disciple. Only Barnabas came to his aid, taking Saul to the apostles so he could share his testimony of what God had done in his life (9:26-27).

> Initially, Christians were afraid of Saul and doubted his sincerity.

Certainly, he had a reputation that extended far and wide. He was no unknown commodity. Not surprisingly, Christians were afraid of him and doubted his sincerity. His conversion was front-page news, indeed! God had brought the biggest enemy of all into His fold!

Paul also mentions Jesus' appearance to him on other occasions. In 1 Corinthians 15:8, he adds it to a list of times that Jesus showed Himself. Literally, Paul calls his appearance a miscarriage or abortion, thereby meaning that it was out of time sequence with the others, coming after the forty day period over which the others occurred (Acts 1:3). In 1 Corinthians 9:1, he bases his apostleship on seeing the risen Lord. He makes other allusions to this event, as well.[14]

Saul the scholar-persecutor had come face to face with Jesus the Lord, the Creator of the universe. In that moment, Saul knew that his vast learning and great zeal were no match for the resurrected Jesus; Saul joined the ranks of those who had similarly been transformed.

APPLICATION

As a direct result of Jesus' resurrection and exaltation, the church was founded, featuring Sunday as the chief day of worship. Lives were changed and thousands became believers through the apostolic preaching. Some of the early church leaders like Peter, James, and Paul experienced profound transformations.

First, if anything can be learned from such a survey, it is that God can work in the most difficult lives, transforming weak believers, skeptical relatives, unbelieving scholars, and outright enemies of the gospel. Today, countless testimonies still witness to God's life-transforming power. The gospel of Jesus Christ, which includes His resurrection, along with God's grace and faith, are the foundations for change.

Second, from each of these transformations we learn something else: God is willing to forgive even major cases of sin.

> God can work in the most difficult lives, transforming weak believers, skeptical relatives, unbelieving scholars, and outright enemies of the gospel.

Whether it was Peter's three forthright denials by a friend, James's blatant unbelief and taunting of his Brother, or Paul's zealous imprisoning and even killing of Christians, God forgave each one. Further, He had a very important place for each of them in the work of His Kingdom. God is a God of compassion and forgiveness.

Third, Christians need to recapture the essence of what inspired these early believers. Now this is certainly not to say that Jesus must appear again in order to transform us; this would be contrary to Jesus' proclamation to Thomas in John 20:29. Rather, believers today are those who trust the testimony of those who saw Jesus. But we can still study and apply the testimonies of those who, after meeting the resurrected Jesus, went out and changed the world. We need to understand more about their motivation, how the knowledge of the gospel so completely changed their lives, and how such information should further inspire us today to be totally sold out to God, as were our early counterparts.

This is largely what this second volume is about. We want the truth of Jesus' resurrection to change every facet of our lives. With Paul, we need to know Him and the power manifested through His resurrection (Phil. 3:10).

NOTES

1. See *The Resurrection: Heart of New Testament Doctrine*, Chapter 3, for our discussion of this subject. For a more detailed discussion, see Gary R. Habermas, *The Resurrection of Jesus: An Apologetic* (Grand Rapids: Baker, 1980; Lanham: University Press of America, 1984), Chapters 2-3.

2. For such a study, see Lowell Streiker, *Mind-Bending: Brainwashing, Cults and Deprogramming in the '80s* (Garden City: Doubleday, 1984).

3. The death of James the brother of John is reported in Acts 12:1-2. Josephus records the martyrdom of James the brother of Jesus in *Antiquities* 20:9. Clement of Rome tells us that Peter and Paul were martyred for their faith (*Corinthians* 5). Further details of these and other deaths are reported by Eusebius (*Ecclesiastical History*, Book II:IX, XXIII, XXV; Book III:XXXI). On the apostles' willingness to die for their faith, see John 21:18-19; Acts 21:13; 25:11; Rom. 14:8; 1 Cor. 15:30-32; 2 Cor. 11:23-32; Phil. 1:20-24; 1 Pet. 1:13-15.

4. See Matt. 28:1,9; Luke 24:1,13; John 20:1,14; cf. Mark 16:1-2; 1 Cor. 15:4, "on the third day."

5. See Acts 20:7; 1 Cor. 16:1-2; cf. Rev. 1:10.

6. See especially Acts 1:15-22; 2:14-42; 3:11-26; 4:8-14; 5:27-33,41-42; 10:9-48; 11:1-18.

7. Acts 1:21-22; 2:22-24,29-33; 3:15,26; 4:10; 10:39-43; cf. 4:2,33.

8. Mark 6:3; 15:40; 16:1; Luke 24:10.

9. We know that this was not James, the apostle and brother of John, since he was martyred earlier by King Herod (Acts 12:1-2).

10. Scholars differ concerning whether or not Gal. 2:1-9 and Acts 15:1-29 describe the same meeting.

11. It may be recalled that Gamaliel was the same scholar who offered the advice that his colleagues accepted with regard to the treatment of Peter and the apostles (Acts 5:33-40).

12. Acts 22:3; 26:5; Phil. 3:5; 1 Tim. 1:12-16.

13. For a discussion of some issues involved here, see the first volume of this set, *The Resurrection: Heart of New Testament Doctrine*, Chapter 5.

14. 1 Tim. 1:12-16; Gal. 1:1,16; Titus 1:3.

SUGGESTED READINGS

Ankerberg, John, and John Weldon. *Do the Resurrection Accounts Conflict? And What Proof Is There That Jesus Rose from the Dead?* Chattanooga: Ankerberg Theological Research Institute, 1990. Pp. 154-165.

Craig, William Lane. *Knowing the Truth about the Resurrection: Our Response to the Empty Tomb*. Revised Edition. Ann Arbor: Servant Books, 1988. Chapter 6.

McDowell, Josh. *The Resurrection Factor*. San Bernardino: Here's Life, 1981. Chapters Seven-Eight.

Tenney, Merrill C. *The Reality of the Resurrection*. New York: Harper and Row, 1963. Chapter VIII.

Reflecting on Lesson One

1. In your own words, what do you think is unique about the transformations of the earliest Christians? Do you agree with the emphasis here on the part played by seeing the resurrected Jesus? Why or why not?

2. In terms of experience alone, how do you compare non-Christian religious testimonies with Christian reports? What are the similarities? What are the differences?

3. Do you think Peter was a Christian prior to meeting the resurrected Jesus? What do you think Jesus meant by what He said to Peter in Luke 22:32?

4. Compare the conversions of James, the brother of Jesus, and Paul. Do you find differences between James, an "internal" critic from within Jesus' own family, and Paul, the external persecutor of the church? What are their similarities?

5. For group discussion: If you had been one of the earliest Christians to hear of Paul's conversion, and even his preaching, how ready would you have been to befriend him? What if you were a group leader and he wanted to address your people? What if you had a family and he asked to stay in your home? Does this give you more respect for what Barnabas did?

6. What other lessons can we learn from the transformations of the early Christians? Name some other areas of application.

Consider this:

Some Christians do not believe evangelism is an activity in which today's church should be engaged. In preparation for Lesson Two research some of their reasons for believing this way. In what ways does the fact of the resurrection impact their logic? Be thinking about how you would counter their viewpoint.

2

EVANGELISM

In this lesson:
- ▶ Case studies of conversion
- ▶ Jesus' command to evangelize
- ▶ The disciples' bold proclamation
- ▶ Different evangelistic strategies with the same message

Fred was definitely a sports junkie. And he didn't just watch games on television. He played ice hockey along with being an amateur boxer. But Fred was also about as far away from Christ as anyone could get.

One night a local preacher showed up at his front door, sent by a good friend who was concerned about Fred. The visit went smoothly until the minister mentioned the subject of sin and everyone's need for salvation. Fred would hear no more. When the preacher continued, Fred had had enough. Standing up and walking over to the chair where the other man sat, Fred ordered him to get out of his house.

"If you don't leave now, I'll pick you up and throw you out the front door!" Fred shouted. Realizing this was no way to lead someone to Christ, the preacher left! But he didn't stay away.

Tactfully, and with help from Fred's friend, the preacher returned on several occasions. Short meetings turned into lunches and then into occasional fishing and golf outings. It was a long, slow process, but after about a year of searching, Fred eventually became a Christian.

"What can I say? I was loved into the Kingdom," he testified later when he started attending the preacher's church. Many of his friends wondered what happened to him. Today Fred still plays sports, but his outings sometimes have other motives, too!

Marie was a successful business woman. She had started her own company and to say that it was doing very well would be an understatement. Her lifestyle began to change, and so did her friends. Expensive clothing, a luxury sports car, and dinner out every night became a way of life. She was happy and successful, but unfulfilled.

"Even though I'm doing just what I want," she told her closest friend, "I feel like I have a hole in my life. I'm fearful that I've seen all there is to the successful life. And the really scary thing is that I'm well aware that my new lifestyle, while very nice, hasn't given me any meaning. I want there to be more — I just don't know what it would look like."

Sitting in a doctor's office one day, she inadvertently picked up a book whose back cover looked interesting. It said something about death and living the good life. Her interest growing the more she read, Marie asked if she could take the book home to read. What impressed her the most was the part that said it was possible to live the good life forever. Later, she got the phone number of the author and called him.

After dozens of phone calls totaling many hours, Marie became a Christian. Totally convinced of the necessity to place God and His Kingdom above all else, she is today a committed believer. Years have gone by, and she has sold her business and "retired." With help from a friend, she selected a number of ministries and gave away a good portion of her wealth. Now she spends most of her time studying, teaching a women's Bible study, and meeting business men and women on a casual basis. Her message to them is almost always the same.

"Money, position, and power do not fulfill," she testifies. "Only in light of eternity do we find the true meaning for which we all long."

One characteristic of the early church that accounts for its continual growth is that the first Christians took very seriously the practice of evangelism. This is evident in at least two ways. The public preaching reported in the

> The first Christians took very seriously the practice of evangelism.

Book of Acts was done by the church leaders. This activity is the chief focus of this chapter.

But on the other hand, the Christian populace was not silent; these individuals also witnessed about their faith. Shortly after Peter's Pentecost sermon when thousands of persons became believers, the activities of the young church were such that unbelievers were attracted. In this case it was apparently the Christian lifestyle that was very enticing to others (Acts 2:42-47, especially v. 47). The indication here is that the Word was spread through friendship and fellowship.

Then, after the persecution of which Saul was a part, the church (with the exception of the apostles) scattered throughout other areas. Wherever these Christians went, they preached the gospel (Acts 8:1,4). So the message continued to spread by word of mouth.

JESUS' COMMAND

The death and resurrection of Jesus Christ were related to early evangelism in at least two important ways. Initially, the catalyst for these witnessing efforts came chiefly by the command of the risen Jesus. Moreover, the message was itself centered in the gospel proclamation.

After Jesus was raised from the dead, He met with His disciples and taught them. His message centered on the Kingdom of God (Acts 1:3), just as it had before the cross. He also commanded His disciples to make the proclamation of the gospel

> After Jesus was raised from the dead, He met with His disciples and taught them.

their chief activity. For example, Luke reports that Jesus rehearsed the nature of the gospel, including His Deity, death, and resurrection, followed by informing the disciples that they were His witnesses of these facts. They were to take this message to all nations, beginning with Jerusalem (Luke 24:45-49).

Before His ascension, Jesus made a similar point. The gospel message was to be taken from Jerusalem, to the surrounding areas, and on to the ends of the earth (Acts 1:8).

Matthew's last message from Jesus to His disciples proclaims that all authority in heaven and earth had been given to Him. Then He told them that He would be with them as they made disciples of people from all nations, baptizing and teaching them (28:18-20). As Matthew's last recorded word the disciples heard from their Master, such a command would have a powerful impact on them.

Later, Peter apparently remembered this moment as he preached the gospel to those who had gathered at Cornelius's home. The apostle mentioned several outstanding facts from Jesus' ministry, including His Deity, death, resurrection, and appearances to the eyewitnesses with whom He ate and drank. Then, Peter recounted, Jesus commanded the disciples to preach the message that He gave them (Acts 10:36-43).

This is the first link in the chain of early Christian evangelism. It came as the risen Jesus commanded the disciples to take His message to all the world, starting with Jerusalem. As He had done, now they were to continue (John 20:21).

THE CENTER OF THE EARLY PROCLAMATION

The second step in early evangelistic efforts was the obedience of the apostles who took every opportunity to publicly proclaim the gospel of Jesus Christ, just as their Teacher had taught them. But they did not do it in their own power. Jesus had promised His presence (Matt. 28:20) and the power of the Holy Spirit (Acts 1:8) in the witnessing effort, which is evident in the results of their preaching.

From the very beginning the key theme was the death and resurrection of Jesus Christ. The Book of Acts is simply filled with proclamations of this nature. In fact, it is mentioned in each of the first five chapters in every discussion, sermon, or confrontation between the apostles and the Jewish leaders.

Beginning with Peter's message on the Day of Pentecost, the Jews were told that they had killed Jesus but that God had raised

Him up again, thereby approving His message (Acts 2:22-24,36). Although David had not yet been raised, Jesus' body did not decay, but He came forth from the grave, appeared to witnesses, and was exalted to the right hand of God (2:29-33).

The Jews were told that they had killed Jesus but that God had raised Him up again, thereby approving His message.

Other texts in this book repeat similar themes. After Peter and John healed a lame man outside of the temple, Peter had another opportunity to preach. Again he boldly confronted his fellow Jews with killing Jesus, noting that God had raised Him from the dead. He and John should have known what they were about: they were eyewitnesses of these events (3:13-15). Later, Peter asserted that God raised Jesus so that the Jews would have a chance to repent (3:26).

Following this last sermon, the Jewish priests, Sadducees, and temple guards were greatly distressed at Peter's and John's testimony and put them in prison. The specific reason for their upset was that the two apostles were teaching the resurrection of both Jesus and the dead. In spite of the imprisonment, the Holy Spirit still blessed the message and many became Christians, increasing the number of male believers to about 5,000 (4:1-4).

But this legal action was not enough to discourage Peter and John. The next day when the Jewish rulers brought them out of prison for questioning, Peter told their accusers directly that they preached by the authority of Jesus Christ, whom the Jews had crucified but God had raised up from the dead (4:10). The apostles were threatened and released.

In another confrontation with the Jewish leaders, the apostles were arrested and jailed. Released by an angel, they returned to their preaching. Brought before the Jewish leaders once again, they were accused of preaching after they were forbidden to do so, attempting to turn the people against the leaders because of their demand for Jesus' death (Acts 5:17-28).

Peter was undaunted by their charge. He directly confronted the Jews with their part in crucifying Jesus, although God had resurrected Him and made them witnesses. This is why they must keep preaching — they

> A legal gag order was not enough to discourage Peter and John.

preferred obedience to God rather than to the Jewish hierarchy (5:30-32). This time, although many of the Jews apparently had had enough and wanted to kill the apostles, they were beaten and released. In a startling passage, the disciples rejoiced that they had suffered in Jesus' name. Then they returned to their preaching (5:33-42)!

We have already mentioned Peter's sermon at Cornelius's home where Jesus' death and resurrection served as the climax of his message (10:39-43). As the case had been before, many listeners were converted (vv. 44;48).

The early chapters of the Book of Acts are clear that the disciples were single-minded in preaching the message of the gospel. At every turn, they missed no opportunity to proclaim the death and resurrection of Jesus Christ. Luke's summary statement says it well: "With great power the apostles continued to testify to the resurrection of the Lord Jesus, and much grace was upon them all" (4:33).

Paul is another apostle who boldly declared the resurrection in the Book of Acts. In a trip to Pisidian Antioch he reported that Jesus had been crucifed by Pilate, thereby fulfilling the

Scriptures. Afterwards, Jesus was buried in a tomb from which He was later raised, appearing to His followers over a period of many days. Through this same Jesus the forgiveness of sins was preached (13:27-43). Several responded to Paul's message.

In our earlier volume, we examined Paul's use of the resurrection with the philosophical skeptics in Acts 17:16-34. We placed more emphasis on vv. 19-34 where Paul made his case before a meeting of the Areopagus philosophers, speaking of the unknown God, the need

> It would be very difficult to emphasize the resurrection more than Paul did!

for repentance, the reality of God's judgment, and the crowning evidence supplied by the resurrection.

But Paul's introduction of the resurrection had first occurred in the local synagogue and marketplace. Paul placed so much emphasis on this act of God that many commentators have remarked that the Greeks apparently thought that he was preaching two gods — Jesus and resurrection (v. 18)! It would be very difficult to emphasize the resurrection more than Paul did! It was this message that gained him an audience before the philosophers of the Areopagus (vv. 19-20,32), after which some believed (v. 34).

Even when Paul stood trial before Agrippa and Festus, he also used the resurrection as the heart of his message. Paul went as far as to assert that his entire debate with the Jewish leaders was over this subject (26:6-8). After reciting his personal testimony of his own meeting with the resurrected Lord Jesus on the way to Damascus (vv. 12-18), Paul declared that his preaching followed that of the Old Testament, which also spoke of the suffering, death, and resurrection of the Christ (vv. 22-23).

It would be difficult to doubt that throughout the entire Book of Acts, the death and resurrection of Jesus Christ formulated the central proclamation. More than once, we are even specifically told that this was the apostolic theme (Acts 4:2,33; 17:18). The purpose was not simply to win a debate, either. As Paul tells us, his purpose was to win people for the Lord — eternity was at stake (2 Cor. 5:11). On numerous occasions, many became believers after hearing the disciples' messages.[1] Just as Jesus had promised (Acts 1:8), the Holy Spirit was indeed present in the apostolic ministry.

APPLICATION

Christians today should be interested in the examples provided for us in the Book of Acts. After all, the apostles were trained by Jesus Himself and were specially guided by the Holy Spirit. What they teach us about the centrality of the gospel of Jesus Christ in the work of evangelism was certainly unique. Further, their methods for accomplishing this task were quite innovative and should serve as a guide for contemporary believers.

First, the gospel needs to remain at the center of both evangelism and biblical preaching, especially to unbelieving audiences. Sometimes it just seems not to be in the forefront of our ministry as much as it was in the New Testament. If the apostolic examples teach us anything, then even the messages that are designed for purposes other than evangelism need to at least incorporate the truth of the gospel. When the disciples stood before the Jewish leaders on more than one occasion, these rulers heard about the cross and the resurrection. And when Paul was on trial

> The gospel needs to remain at the center of both evangelism and biblical preaching, especially to unbelieving audiences.

for his life before Agrippa and Festus, he proclaimed this theme. The apostles got the message across in a variety of ways, even when they stood before the legal authorities, leaving no question about the single-minded purpose of their preaching.

So like their Master before them,[2] Jesus' pupils were experts at turning conversations and other opportunities into discussions of the gospel. Other instances are not hard to find. Whether it was Peter addressing the crowd that gathered out of curiosity, having observed the results of the Holy Spirit's coming at Pentecost, or Peter and John seizing the moment afforded by the multitude that gathered to observe the lame man who had been healed, the gospel just naturally moved to the forefront of the discussions. Paul in the Jewish synagogue, the marketplace, then before the philosophers of the Areopagus are other examples. Normal conversation didn't just include the death and resurrection of Jesus Christ, but *centered* on them, whether or not they started out that way.

Early Christian leaders continually spoke about the death and resurrection because it was of primary importance to them.

The reason why these early Christian leaders continually spoke about this subject is evident: it was of primary importance to them. This should say something about our own interests and make us question whether the gospel is just as crucial for us. It is simply normal to talk about what is foremost on our minds.

Second, Paul's typical method in Acts 13–19 presents an innovative technique for church planting. He often entered local Jewish synagogues to witness about the Messiah. We are told that his *normal custom* was to "reason," "argue," or even "prove" from the Old Testament Scriptures that Jesus was the Christ, including a presentation of His death and resurrection.[3] Those who belived in each city gathered together as a new local church.

Not only is such an apologetic strategy a "lost art" in church planting today, but many Christians are even outspokenly opposed to such methods. I sometimes hear believers say that reasoning, arguing, debating, and the like have no place in witnessing. But this attitude should be reassessed unless we are prepared to question Paul's technique.[4]

However, this does not mean that all debate scenarios are therefore allowable. It is certainly conceivable, for instance, that arguing or debating could otherwise be offensive in ways never intended by Paul. In the wrong context, they can be very hurtful.[5] But the opposite is also the case — the Bible not only allows such efforts when they are done in the right circumstances, but even endorses them by presenting them in a straightforward manner, including recording the conversions that took place. To embrace the alternative position presents biblical problems.

Some might make a lesser charge, however. Perhaps Paul ministered in this way because of the better opportunity it afforded to reach the Jews in these cities, but the need for such today is minimized. But used similarly, maybe this technique would be most helpful for building a ministry among those who profess different religious beliefs, or with persons who have other common characteristics with these New Testament audiences, like college students or professionals. While debate is certainly not the only method used by the apostles to plant churches,[6] it still could be fruitful today.

Third, it should not go unnoticed that Paul used different methods, depending on whom he was addressing. Paul acknowledged this in 1 Corinthians 9:19-23. While always preaching the

Paul used different meth-
ods, depending on whom
he was addressing.

same gospel, without any
change in content, the
means by which he presented it varied.

For example, with Jews,
Paul was much more likely to argue from the Old Testament in
order to show that Jesus was the Messiah (Acts 13:32-39; 17:2-3).
With Greeks, Paul would speak about their own situation, citing
their own writers or the way God worked in nature (Acts 14:15-17;
17:22-31), usually working his way to a discussion of Jesus' resurrection (Acts 17:31; cf. 26:12-18,23). This distinction makes sense
because the Jews, of course, accepted the Old Testament while
the Greeks did not. With both groups, Paul's messages of Jesus
Christ's Deity, death, and resurrection remained central.

This would seem to indicate that we, likewise, should adapt
our method to the differences in modern listeners. Approaches
that worked with unbelievers a generation ago might not be
appropriate for more recent discussions. But we must always
allow the same gospel to remain the chief message that we
need to get across.

In these and other ways, we can learn from the evangelistic
strategies utilized in the early church. We can keep the gospel
central in our preaching, teaching, and discussions, as well as look
for ways to turn the topic in that direction whenever possible. Many
witnessing strategies are consistent with those in the early church,
but this does not preclude being open to innovative church planting techniques, being certain to keep the same message.

Fourth, I think believers need to reevaluate their motivation
for evangelism. Do we engage in it solely because we have to do
so? It is true that it is a command from our Lord and this should
affect our passion to witness for Him. But perhaps our perspective needs to change even more.

In our first volume, we discussed the "top-down principle," which is the biblical admonition to view life and its various aspects from the perspective of God and His eternal Kingdom. We made some suggestions on how we might apply this to our problems, ministries, relationships,

> Believers need to reevaluate their motivation for evangelism.

and so on. The key idea is that life from the standpoint of eternity provides a new motivation for simple living. For example, laying up treasures in heaven, as commanded by Jesus, can be related to evangelism. We are told that those we lead to Christ are our "crown" (1 Thess. 2:19-20).[7]

Another perspective is to view the same question from the unsaved persons' angle. If eternal life is the greatest gift in the world, as I believe it is, then shouldn't our love for others want them to share an eternal future with their Creator? Even if they seem not to appreciate our efforts on their behalf, should even that keep us from wanting the best for them? So a heavenly perspective dictates that one motivation for evangelism is the love of others and a desire for them to share heaven, too.

NOTES

1. See Acts 2:41; 4:4; 10:44-48; 13:43; 17:1-4; 17:34.

2. Jesus modeled this ability often, as we see in His discussions with Nicodemus (John 3:3-5,15), the Samaritan woman at the well (John 4:1-42), and Martha (John 11:21-27).

3. The clearest statement of this practice is Acts 17:2-3. Other examples are Acts 14:1; 19:8.

4. Some Christians have even gone as far as to argue that, on these occasions, Paul was actually out of God's will and guilty of preaching in the flesh! They sometimes cite texts like 1 Cor. 2:1-2 to say that Paul had abandoned

his older methods. But several things should be briefly noted in response. First, in each of the Acts passages, Paul was presenting the gospel. To deny this is to mistake his *method* for his *content*. The latter did not change. Second, this objection exposes very questionable hermeneutical practices. Since Scripture *never* tells us that Paul was mistaken here, are we then also free to doubt other teachings such as Paul's view of women? This should be troublesome for those who hold to the docrine of the inerrancy of Scripture. Third, why would 1 Cor. 2:1-2 disallow Paul's earlier use of evidence when presenting the gospel? In 1 Cor. 15, which was written after the episodes in Acts occurred, the objector would have to conclude that Paul slipped again, reverting to the use of evidence for Jesus' resurrection! Fourth, in the cases in Acts, listeners were almost always converted after Paul's presentation, indicating the promised activity of the Holy Spirit. There is no clue whatsoever that this was simply a case of God's Word not returning void. In sum, this challenge to Paul's methodology appears to be both without biblical support and otherwise faulty on its own grounds.

5. For example, sometimes argument is engaged in for its own sake, or for one's ego. Other times, unbelievers are invited onto the believer's turf, perhaps into a church, as wolves among the sheep. (It should be noticed that Paul was always in the territory of unbelievers when debating with them.) Whenever such methods are employed, we should be very sensitive to avoid circumstances that may cause some Christians to experience doubt concerning their faith. Even if the Christian apologist prevails in the dialogue, this does not mean that no damage to believers occurred. It may be the first time that sensitive Christians have heard someone attack Christianity. The questions sometimes remain in their minds long after they are thoroughly answered. Paul was also concerned about these occasions, reporting that the faith of some had even been destroyed in what might have been similar circumstances. So he condemned the wrong use of arguing in contexts that may have included disputing doctrine (2 Tim. 2:16-18; cf. 1 Tim. 6:20-21). I think whether the situation is biblical or not depends to a large extent on how it is done.

6. Our earlier point may be recalled that Peter built the church at Jerusalem into the largest of that time by his preaching, a much more common method today.

7. On the ethical and unethical senses of seeking rewards, see Habermas, *The Resurrection: Heart of Christian Doctrine,* Chapter 6: "A Foretaste of Heaven." For more on this subject, see Gary R. Habermas and J.P. Moreland, *Beyond Death: Exploring the Evidence for Immortality* (Wheaton, IL: Crossway Books, 1998), Chapter 15.

Resurrection: Heart of the Christian Life   42

SUGGESTED READINGS

Boice, James Montgomery. *The Christ of the Empty Tomb.* Chicago: Moody Press, 1985.

Green, Michael. *The Empty Cross of Christ.* Downers Grove, IL: InterVarsity, 1984. Chapter 12.

Little, Paul E. *How to Give Away Your Faith.* Downers Grove, IL: InterVarsity, 1966.

Kennedy, D. James. *Evangelism Explosion.* Third Edition. Wheaton, IL: Tyndale House, 1970.

Sparrow-Simpson, W.J. *The Resurrection and the Christian Faith.* Grand Rapids: Zondervan, 1911, reprint 1968. Chapters XV-XVI.

Reflecting on Lesson Two

1. What do the testimonies of Fred and Marie at the beginning of this chapter say about pushing harder even when an unsaved person opposes us?

2. Do you find any importance in the fact that, after His resurrection, Jesus continued His central message of the Kingdom of God and how to get there? In other words, what significance is there that Jesus' chief topic stayed the same?

3. Why do you think that the message given by the resurrected Jesus to His followers included a command to make disciples of others by teaching and preaching the gospel?

4. How can believers ensure that the gospel is always our central message? What are some ways we might be tempted to get away from it to other themes that, while important, are secondarily so? What can we do to make sure that these other concerns do not take the place of the gospel?

5. For group discussion: When do you think that debates and the public use of apologetics are needed as a method for spreading the gospel? When (and where) are these not such good ideas? What concerns do you have? How can they be answered?

6. For group discussion: Can you think of some innovative methods of witnessing that are especially attuned to the needs of a certain group of people? Give some specific examples.

7. Group action project: Take at least one example from the last question and actually implement it. In what situation would it work the best? Coffee House? Public debate? Public lecture on a "hot" topic related to the gospel? Door-to-door? After-school Bible study? A community project where sharing your faith is allowed? Then pick a time and try it out.

8. Does the top-down perspective provide you with a different angle on evangelism? Does the prospect of laying up treasures in heaven give you any motivation? What about loving the unsaved person enough to want them to spend eternity in heaven, too? Which one do you find to be more motivating? Why?

Consider this:

Have you ever doubted your salvation? the existence of God? the truth of Christianity? Under what circumstances are you most likely to face serious doubts about your faith? How did you overcome these doubts? Consider how the resurrection could calm those thoughts and strengthen your faith.

3

CHRISTIAN DOUBT

In this lesson:

▶ The common occurrence of doubt
▶ Different kinds of doubt
▶ How Jesus dealt with doubters
▶ Different approaches to different doubts

Any of Kathy's friends would have said that she was an excellent Christian. She spent two hours every day in personal devotions. But somehow she began to entertain the idea that she was unsaved. The more she thought about it, the more nervous she felt. Within a relatively short period of time, she was having anxiety attacks. She stopped reading her Bible because she thought it was aggravating the situation. Finally, she concluded that God was using her emotions to warn her that she was unsaved.

When Philip first came to talk about doubt, he couldn't believe that he was a Christian or that God loved him. Physically abused as a child, with a recent operation to prove it, he struggled with the thought that anyone loved him. Neither his obvious intelligence nor his college degree in philosophy had rescued him from the painful ravages of doubt. He began to call me late into the night, beginning with the words, "It's me again. Do you have a few minutes?" I knew better. He grew more argumentative and angry the longer we talked. But there was no denying the amount of pain he was experiencing. What he wanted most in life — to be sure he was loved by God — had totally eluded him. "Will I ever have peace?" he asked regularly.

What is doubt? Did biblical characters also experience it? How do we handle it? What relationship is there between Jesus' resurrection and uncertainty? This is a multifaceted issue and cannot be dealt with here in as much depth as is necessary, but we will at least attempt to shed a little light on a painful and complicated problem.[1]

THE NATURE OF DOUBT

At least seven Greek words are translated in the New Testament as "doubt" or a synonym. The words can indicate unbelief, uncertainty, despair, or hesitation between belief and unbelief. In this chapter we will deal with Christians and their struggles, defining doubt as a lack of certainty concerning the teachings of Christianity or one's relation to them.

Doubt is a very broad subject, extending far beyond what are possibly its two most common questions — whether Christianity

is true and gaining assurance concerning our own faith. This subject also includes topics like why God does not answer prayer as
we think He should or why we suffer as we do. Uncertainty is far-
reaching and, in one form or another, has probably touched the
lives of virtually all believers.

> Doubt is a very broad subject, extending far
> beyond what are possibly its two most common
> questions — whether Christianity is true and
> gaining assurance concerning our own faith.

We doubt because we are humans — because of our sinful and
finite natures. We have rebelled against God, thereby affecting
our relationship with Him. Our finite natures keep us from knowing everything. Combined, we have a recipe for uncertainty.

Interestingly, unbelievers also doubt! They may also wonder,
for instance, whether Christianity just might be true after all, or
if they are as sure about their position as they would like to think.
After recounting his own struggle with doubt, C.S. Lewis added,
"when I was an atheist I had moods in which Christianity looked
terribly probable."[2]

It would be a mistake to think that there is only one kind of
doubt. I think it is helpful to speak of three different species: factual, emotional, and volitional. Factual doubt may be caused, for
example, by questions that concern the truth of Christianity, like
the existence of God, evidence for a miracle, or the basis for
accepting Scripture. When the issue is adequately addressed,
this variety of uncertainty should subside.

Emotional doubt is by far the most common of the three
types, as well as being the most painful. It basically arises from

our feelings and is more subjective in its perspective, often being mood-related. A very common example is the assurance of salvation, with the individual asking if they really trusted Jesus Christ. Quite regularly, "What if . . . ?" questions fuel the fires of emotional doubt, apart from any real reason to believe there is a problem. "I know that, but *what if* I'm not a believer?" Distraught psychological states are not uncommon.

Volitional doubt is related to our will, motivation, and the choices we make. Here the chief concerns might be strengthening our faith, applying truth to our life, or our motivation to follow God.

Just like various physical illnesses require different sorts of medical treatments, so the healing of different types of doubt also requires the proper approach. Applying the right corrective presupposes properly identifying the kind of uncertainty that is involved.

Further, since we all have intellect, emotions, and will, our doubts are also frequently of a compound nature. Neither we nor our doubts can always be divided up into nice, neat categories. In cases of compound doubt, just like physical illnesses, the dominant form of uncertainty is often the one causing the most discomfort and it needs to be treated. Issues like these make doubt a complicated matter. However, not only does Scripture present a variety of examples of doubting saints, but it also supplies us with some strong answers. Jesus confronted doubt head-on, indicating some directions for us to follow.

JESUS CONFRONTS DOUBT

In our first volume, we saw that Jesus frequently dealt with persons who experienced doubt or other questions. These var-

ied quite widely, from unbelievers like the Jewish spiritual leaders who occasionally asked for a sign and James the brother of
Jesus, to believers like John the Baptist. After Jesus' resurrection,
all of His disciples apparently experienced some doubt, as we
will see.

Perhaps it would be helpful to categorize some of the ques-
tioners who spoke to Jesus, to see how He dealt with them.
Thomas is best considered to be a factual doubter since he
required evidence and, when it was provided, he was satisfied
(John 20:24-29). Paul might have been in this class, too, since it
would be difficult to imagine that he did not have any questions.
But the appearances of the risen Jesus to each of these men
overwhelmed them, answering everything at once!

It would seem that John the Baptist's uncertainty was of the
emotional variety, given his circumstances: he was in prison, isolated from his friends and loved ones, and kept from his ministry.
Perhaps he even sus-
pected that he would
lose his life. He sent
his disciples to Jesus
with serious ques-
tions. Given his prior

> John the Baptist's uncertainty
> was of the emotional variety,
> prompted by his circumstances.

ministry, along with his unwavering strength and commitment to
God, we see how even a strong believer can have times of
uncertainty (Luke 7:18-28). Although we cannot be sure, it would
seem that James, the brother of Jesus, must also have experienced some emotional doubt as he witnessed some of the
incredible things that were said about his Brother (cf. John 7:3-5).

The Jewish leaders and others who harassed Jesus, asking for
signs on several occasions,[3] are examples of volitional doubters.
James probably had some of these questions, too. In each case,

these individuals appeared to be aware of Jesus' ministry, including His preaching and His miracles, and at least the Jewish leaders heard Jesus' prediction of His own resurrection from the dead. That they witnessed so much is an indication of their choice not to believe; they willed their state of unbelief.

How did Jesus deal with each of these doubters? He treated factual doubters such as Thomas and Paul (if he is placed here) by answering their request for evidence. When Thomas said that the testimony of his fellow apostles was insufficient for him to believe, Jesus appeared to him personally. Paul also met Jesus directly. In each case, the evidence was enough to overcome their uncertainty, although Jesus told Thomas it would have been better for him not to have required the appearance in order to believe (John 20:29).

Although John the Baptist may also have experienced some factual doubt (especially if he never witnessed any of Jesus' miracles for himself), it appears that his uncertainty was chiefly emotional. And once again, Jesus provided John with evidence to show that He was the promised Messiah, along with a word of encouragement for him to remain firm in his faith (Luke 7:21-23). Presumably, any emotional needs that James had were properly and personally dealt with during Jesus' private postresurrection appearance to him, although details are not provided.

With those affected by volitional uncertainty, Jesus preached and once again offered evidence for His claims. He predicted His resurrection as the chief indication that His teachings were truthful (see above). This is as far as Jesus could minister to the Jewish leaders who asked for a sign, since they willed not to believe. Like the brothers of the rich man in Jesus' story, people can refuse to exercise faith even if someone appears to them after death (Luke 16:27-31). With James, whose doubt also seems to have been volitional, Jesus appeared to him personally and solved his dilemma (1 Cor. 15:7). This conclusion is evident from James's later commitment and leadership in the early church, as well as from his epistle; faith and motivation were no longer problems for him.[4]

So Jesus was faced by different forms of uncertainty along with the various personality types who manifested them. He did not neglect any of them, but dealt with each according to their own individual needs. But after His resurrection, He perhaps faced the most widespread case of doubt — that expressed by His own disciples who did not believe that He had been raised from the dead.

One strange aspect of the disciples' doubt is that Jesus had, on many occasions, told them that He would die and afterwards rise again.[5] But despite how many times He repeated this prediction, they were simply not prepared for it. In Matthew 16:22-23, Peter rebuked Jesus for saying this and was rebuked by Jesus, in turn. A few times we are told that the disciples just did not understand Jesus' prediction (Mark 9:32; Luke 18:34; John 2:22). In Mark 14:27-28, Peter objected a second time, to be greeted by Jesus' prediction of his denials.

Further, Jesus told the disciples to meet Him in Galilee after His death and resurrection (Mark 14:27-28), but they didn't go there until the risen Jesus repeated His message to them personally (Matt. 28:7; Mark 16:7-8).

> The disciples thought the women were spreading false stories.

Even after the resurrection, but before they saw Jesus, they apparently did not realize that they would see Him alive (John 20:9; Luke 24:20-21). When the women reported their experiences at the empty tomb, the disciples thought they were spreading false stories (Luke 24:11).

This confusion continued even after the disciples personally met the risen Jesus. On the first Easter Sunday when Jesus appeared, Luke tells us that His followers were startled, thinking that they had seen a ghost. Jesus responded by asking them, "Why are you troubled, and why do doubts rise in your minds?" (Luke 24:36-38). Then Jesus showed Himself to the disciples to demonstrate that He had risen in His own body. He even ate with them (vv. 39-43), reminding them that all of this was supposed to happen (vv. 44-46).

Later when Jesus appeared to his disciples in Galilee, according to His promise, the disciples worshiped Him. But we are also told that even here, some of them doubted (Matt. 28:17)! The Greek word here (*edistasan*) is not unbelief, but the hesitation that we spoke of above. In all fairness, this possibly refers to others who were present besides the apostles. After all, Jesus had directed His followers to this mountain ahead of time (v. 16) and the word could well have gotten around.

The disciples' variety of doubt was probably factual in nature. Their uncertainty did not seem to be caused primarily by emotions, although these surely came into play after the death of their best friend. Neither does it appear to be a case of their having the will not to believe — in fact, it might be said that they really wanted to do so with all of their hearts, as indicated by their joy at realizing that it was truly Jesus (John 20:20).

> The disciples' variety of doubt was probably factual in nature.

It just took a meeting or two with the disciples for everyone to be absolutely sure that they were not just "seeing things." So while the others did not go as far as Thomas in their doubting, some uncertainty was apparent. There were probably even some people who were present at each of the appearances who had not seen the risen Jesus before. This may be what Paul meant by "all the apostles" in 1 Corinthians 15:7 or the presence of 120 people in Acts 1:15. The "newcomers" would have to be allowed their time of hesitation, too!

Jesus seemed to understand their uncertainty. His disciples believed it was He (John 20:20), but their joy was mixed with doubt (Luke 24:41). Like His response to the other cases, He used His resurrection appearances to answer their uncertainty. The strategy worked, for the third time Jesus appeared to the disciples, with seven of them present, no one asked any questions — they knew it was Jesus (John 21:12-14).

We can summarize Jesus' overall strategy with doubters: He faced it directly. With hardened unbelievers He decried their requirement of proof and warned them of judgment. Knowing their hearts, He was aware that they would not believe no matter how much evidence they received. Some would simply refuse to convert even if they had seen Jesus alive (Luke 16:29-31). Yet He still promised His resurrection as a sign, even to these persons. They were not without a witness.

Regarding John the Baptist's doubt, Jesus sent a report of his miracles back with John's disciples and encouraged him to remain firm. With the apostles, including Thomas, James, and Paul, doubts and questions were greeted by resurrection appearances along with personal messages to those involved. He showed His resurrected body to Thomas, yet He did give him a mild rebuke for not believing sooner. We are not told what Jesus said to His brother James. Jesus challenged Paul for his persecution of believers. After the initial shock, the meetings with His disciples were cordial, even warm, as well as being learning sessions.

One of the interesting lessons here is that Jesus did not fail to provide the unbelieving Jews with a sign even though He knew that they wouldn't believe. At least two of the individuals who saw the resurrected Jesus (James and Paul) were also unsaved before they met Him. The different treatment is due, it seems clear, to the heart conditions of those involved. Jesus treated everyone personally and according to their particular condition.

> Jesus did not fail to provide the unbelieving Jews with a sign even though He knew that they wouldn't believe.

I think we often forget the tremendous effect that Jesus' resurrection appearances had on those who witnessed them. But what could possibly have done more to alleviate doubt, if the persons were at least open to God's working? To witness the risen Jesus appearing in His glorified body must have been so totally overwhelming that it just dissolved the doubt.

This was the effect on Thomas. He changed instantly from a position of skepticism, stating that he would not believe his friends' testimony, to belief, followed by openly worshiping Jesus. And then there was Paul — the famous persecutor who certainly met his match in the risen and glorified Jesus. Never looking back again, he could do nothing but a total about-face, perhaps becoming the most accomplished theologian and missionary in the history of the church. After seeing Jesus alive, James, too, went from an unbeliever who taunted Jesus to the pastor of the largest ancient church.

Jesus presented a live object lesson to counter doubts. Although these appearances ended after forty days, we can still study the eyewitness testimony, which is still available. The result can also be the conquering of our doubt in the twenty-first century.

But does this mean that Jesus always used evidences to address doubt? Again, knowing the people to whom He was speaking, He did employ other means when needed. Sometimes He taught them (Luke 24:25-27,44-49; Matt. 28:18-20). After being questioned regarding why He hadn't come sooner and kept her brother from dying, Jesus also instructed Martha (John 11:20-27). Here, He addressed her emotional grief. We will note His strategy in the next chapter.

In sum, Jesus knew the needs of those He was addressing; even more, He knew and understood the depths of their hearts. Accordingly, He differentiated between each of those with whom he spoke. His measured responses were more than any merely human counselor could provide, for while we attempt to ascertain what species of doubt (and perhaps a combination) is involved in each case, Jesus could cut through all of the theory. We could learn much from His insights into this subject, including interweaving His resurrection along with other techniques, like those Jesus employed. Jesus made unique contributions to the issue of uncertainty and we can profit from such methods.

APPLICATION

The issue of religious doubt is complicated and multifaceted. Most (if not all) believers suffer from it in some way, at some time. Even if it is not a pleasant topic, much can be learned from studying it. There are many worthwhile lessons to apply.

The first matter for application is to realize that doubt is not an isolated phenomenon, even among biblical saints. It is much more common than we may think. Many times we find typical sorts of uncertainty expressed by biblical characters, perhaps questioning the prospering of the wicked or the like. In a fair number of cases, a believer cries out, complaining to God in very strong language. Such emotional doubt is expressed by believers like Job, various psalmists, Jeremiah, and Habakkuk.[6]

Doubt, even among biblical saints, is much more common than we may think.

Frequently, the faulty thinking is corrected, sometimes in the same passage where the doubts are expressed. Either God or even the writer himself counters the charge with the truth.[7] This does not excuse crying out against God, but it does show that spiritually-minded individuals have frequently struggled with their emotions.

Second, we should note that believers often tell themselves all sorts of untruths about the subject of doubt. We have just seen an example. It is not true that spiritual people never face doubt. We have seen that it occurs to both Old and New Testament saints. So Christians today have no basis for concluding that they are the only ones going through it. That other believers frequently doubt does not excuse it, but it does show that we are not alone (1 Cor. 10:13).

Uncertainty is not necessarily the opposite of faith, either. Rather, it usually consists of questioning or hesitating between two options. It is not unbelief in and of itself. Further, doubt is not necessarily sin. John the Baptist was not reprimanded for his questions but was even praised by the Lord during the same time that he suffered his uncertainty. Others turned their doubt into victory.

Neither are all doubts treated the same way. Different types require different methods, even as our Lord reacted variously to those in need. And we can have an improper conception about the overall subject, just as we can about the individual parts. Therefore, correcting our misplaced thinking about doubt is the proper starting point in conquering it. Recognizing our faulty beliefs reminds us that we must apply truth to this subject. Few lessons help send us on the road to victory more surely than weeding out our poor thinking here. Just as sickness requires the proper medicine, so we need the right application with our uncertainty.

Third, Jesus knew the hearts of those to whom He was speaking. So He was able to deal with each case according to the needs of the individual. He knew just when to continue a discussion and when to cut it off. He knew who would be affected and who would not, no matter what was done or said. Not having the same abilities, believers need to be open to the work of the Holy Spirit and to know more about the various types of uncertainty and how to deal with them. This concern has taken books to express, so we cannot hope to do justice to it here. But a few ideas may still be helpful either for the doubter or for those who are trying to help them.

With factual uncertainty, the primary concern is having the data needed to answer the particular questions. Therefore, providing a solid foundation is of foremost importance. A strong temptation here is getting sidetracked on peripheral issues. For example, differing views on the date of creation, which version of the Bible to read, various forms of church government, or eschatological theories are important, but do not need to be solved in order for a believer to obtain peace. Christians have numerous possible

> With factual uncertainty, the primary concern is having the data needed to answer the particular questions.

options that can be held on such subjects while still remaining within biblical parameters. However, the gospel concerning the Person of Jesus Christ, His atoning death, and resurrection are of utmost concern. Happily, it is precisely these crucial topics that are the best evidenced.[8]

Believers should follow the lead of Jesus Himself, who offered His resurrection not only as the primary indication of the truthfulness of His message but also as the chief answer to doubt. Believers have not been as faithful in applying this event to doubt issues as they have been in arguing for its historicity.

Fourth, emotional uncertainty is not only the most common and painful type, but is probably the trickiest with which to deal, too. I am not a psychologist, psychiatrist, or professional counselor. But there are plenty of good sources for treating emotional struggles in general, some of which are either side effects or causes of doubt.[9] One example in Jesus' ministry was that of John the Baptist. Another was His discussion with Martha.

In other passages of Scripture we find more details. In Philippians 4:6-9 the topic is anxiety (a very common ingredient in emotional doubt), providing Paul's advice for dealing with it. He encourages believing prayer (v. 6) that gives the problem to God (cf. 1 Pet. 5:7) and thanksgiving to God (v. 6). Then he tells his readers to substitute edifying thoughts in place of our anxious ones (v. 8). Lastly, they were to regularly practice these principles (v. 9).[10]

Each of these steps has the potential to cut short our emotional suffering. For instance, thanksgiving to God in the middle of a problem can change our mood almost immediately. On dozens of occasions, I have asked audiences how many of them have spent as much as ten minutes either praising or thanking God during a particularly emotional time. Many hands are always extended into the air. Then I ask what happens to the mood when they do this. Without an exception, someone calls out: "The mood changes." "Is this your experience?" I ask. Heads all over the room are shaken up and down in agreement. This step alone has relieved much pain.

Even so, perhaps the key here is changing our thinking from thoughts that cause anxiety (or depression) to ones that are wholesome and truthful (v. 8). This cannot be emphasized too strongly: the doubt-causing thoughts must be forcibly confronted and substituted with the truth. The reason here is simple. If our anxious thoughts cause worry, then changing those thoughts will bring relief.

> The key is changing our thinking from thoughts that cause anxiety to ones that are wholesome and truthful.

William Backus and Marie Chapian encourage a similar method called "Misbelief Therapy," where the person moves through three steps in order to change their emotionally painful thoughts. We must locate the wrong thoughts ("lies") that we are telling ourselves, remove them by arguing against them ("That thought is not true because . . . ."), and replace them with truthful, biblical thoughts.[11]

Applied to emotional doubt, Christians should attack and replace untrue thoughts like, "What if Christianity is not true after all?" Or, "What if, after all is said and done, I'm not truly saved? What if I didn't say the right words?" Emotional uncertainty most typically centers on the slight chance that one may be mistaken in some (often unidentified) way. But as Paul explains, this thinking must not only be weeded out and replaced by true thoughts, but this corrective process should be practiced until it becomes a habit (Phil. 2:8-9).

So instead of questioning the truth of Christianity, one might think, "Dozens of factual data prove the truthfulness of my faith," reviewing any number of individual arguments as needed. Just as Jesus applied His miracles to John the Baptist's emotional struggles, so evidences can provide a starting point for over-coming this kind of doubt. Or when a Christian is tempted to wonder if they are saved, they might concentrate on the truth-fulness of the gospel and the reality of their own choice to trust the Lord.

Kathy learned after talking to a friend that she had no good reason to question her salvation. She had done exactly what the New Testament said she should do for her salvation. To hammer this point home, she found it helpful to reduce the subject to two questions: (1) Are the gospel facts true? (2) Did I surrender in faith to the Jesus Christ of the gospel? She never really strug-gled with the first question; besides, she knew these issues were solved by a study of the evidences. But the second one was much tougher for her. But she stuck with it and made herself stay on track. "Yes," she began to say *forcefully* to herself. "I *did* trust Jesus Christ by faith." By repeating this process *whenever the doubts came*, she learned to control them. It wasn't always easy, but she refused to allow her mind to wander to "What ifs" or other issues. The more she concentrated on the truth, the stronger she became.

"Now I have an idea of how to apply biblical truth," she delightedly told her friend.

The key in emotional doubt is to figure out the untruths we are telling ourselves and correct the unbiblical thinking. This can be tough — like pulling weeds — but the final victory is unspeak-ably rewarding. The process is taught in Scripture and it actually works![12]

Phillip's chief problem was that, for some reason, he was scared to apply this process to his doubts concerning God's love. We talked for many hours, but to no avail. Then he would get angry with God and start all over again with his doubts. One night he stopped by to talk again. I decided I had to get firm with him, since we had probably reviewed the strategy at least a dozen times, but he hadn't tried it even once.

"I'm going to go over the process one more time with you. If you don't at least try to apply it, there is absolutely no need to continue talking about it." I reviewed the steps one at a time, making sure he understood.

The next time I saw Phillip, he was radiant. He had applied the techniques. Surprise! They had really worked! Encouraged by the success and release from his pain, he kept applying the biblical balm whenever needed. After almost fifteen years, he's not only doing fine. As an elder in his church, he has had many opportunities to lead others to the same victory!

Fifth, concerning volitional doubt, Jesus' work was often shortened by His supernatural knowledge of the hardened unbelief of some of His listeners. The New Testament also has much to say about our will and activating it in a proper way. Repentance from our neglect of God's Word and commitment to Him are the starting points. Then we need to change our thinking, just as we described above. But volitional doubt requires an additional foundation. It needs something to inspire it to action.

> Volitional doubt requires an additional foundation—something to inspire it to action.

We have said in both of these volumes that the biblical model for motivation comes from seeking God and His Kingdom first, above all else (Matt. 6:33). What could be better than living the good life for eternity? If eternal life with the God of the universe and with other believers cannot inspire us, we need to meditate deeply on Christian truth, allowing it to sink into our minds. This outlook needs to be activated precisely *during* our doubts and trials. The purpose is to bring our will into conformity with God's and to be motivated to follow Him wholeheartedly.[13]

I have seen these methods work over and over again, even in tough cases. In fact, I have never had anyone maintain that they had tried these biblical steps without getting substantial relief from their struggles. What I do hear repeatedly is that *they work whenever they are applied.* Unfortunately, the person often goes on to say that they don't always make the best effort to apply them, even when they are hurting! I guess a person just needs to decide how much they want to get over it!

This is not to say that no other methods will work. Other suggestions can also be applied with great success, also with support from Scripture. Sometimes medical treatment may be necessary. We are just providing a few of the biblical paths that can be applied to the dilemma of doubt.

Sixth, doubt can be serious. Even if it is frequently found in Scripture and is common among believers, it must be taken care of when it affects our lives and relationship with the Lord. Doubt prevention measures

> Regular prayer and other doubt prevention measures are helpful in keeping uncertainty from gaining a foothold.

like regular prayer, Scripture study, fellowship with other believers, and especially Christian meditation on God's truths are especially helpful in keeping uncertainty from gaining a foothold in our lives.

Sometimes doubt starts with factual questions. If these are not dealt with, it may progress to our emotions, where constant defeats may affect our volition. Here, like a cancer, it can deaden our motivation and will to serve God. This is why volitional doubt is perhaps the most serious species. We must be alert to dangers like these, as well as being on the lookout for its affect on other believers. Helping to rescue those who are hurting from the pangs of doubt, by God' s grace, is a great accomplishment (Jas. 5:19-20). Having to confront another Christian about losing their will to serve and seek the Lord may not be enjoyable, but it may spare them God's judgment (Jude 22-23). And we must also constantly examine our own lives and our own thinking, as well (1 Cor. 10:12).

NOTES

1. For more in-depth treatments, see Os Guinness, *In Two Minds: The Dilemma of Doubt and How to Resolve It* (Downers Grove, IL: InterVarsity, 1976). This book was reissued as *Doubt* (Batavia, IL: Lion Publishing, 1987). See also Gary R. Habermas, *The Thomas Factor: Using Your Doubts to Grow Closer to God* (Nashville: Broadman and Holman, 1999) and *Dealing with Doubt* (Chicago: Moody, 1990).

2. C.S. Lewis, *Mere Christianity* (New York: Macmillan, 1952), p. 123; cf. pp. 122–124.

3. Matt. 12:38-40; 16:1-4; John 2:18-22; 6:26-33; 10:24-26.

4. But this is not to say that only unbelievers can be volitional doubters. Many Christians suffer from weak faith or are plagued by the seeming inability to apply teachings to their lives or are not motivated to fully commit themselves to God. They, too, can change, but often do not.

5. For just a few of these examples, see Mark 9:31-32; 14:27-28; Luke 18:31-34; John 2:18-22.

6. For just a few examples, see Job 7:11; 10:3-4,13-14,20-22; 12:6; 13:21; 14:6; 19:7; 27:2; Ps. 44:9-26; 60:1; 82:2; 89:38-39; Jer. 12:1-4; 14:8-9; 15:18; 20:7; Hab. 1–2.

7. With the texts in endnote 6, compare Job 38–42, especially 38:1-4; 40:1-5; 42:1-6; Ps. 42, especially vv. 5-11; 43, especially vv. 4-5; 60:12; 89:52; Jer. 12:14-17; 16:19-21; 20:13; Hab. 3.

8. It is not the purpose of these two volumes to provide an apologetic argument for Christianity. For those interested in the factual basis of the gospel and other essential doctrines, there are many good overviews that are highly recommended. See, for examples, William Lane Craig, *Reasonable Faith* (Westchester: Crossway Books, 1994); Norman Geisler, *Christian Apologetics* (Grand Rapids: Baker, 1976); A.J. Hoover, *The Case for Christian Theism: An Introduction to Apologetics* (Grand Rapids: Baker, 1976); J.P. Moreland, *Scaling the Secular City: A Defense of Christianity* (Grand Rapids: Baker, 1987); Ronald H. Nash, *Faith and Reason: Searching for a Rational Faith* (Grand Rapids: Zondervan, 1988); Terry L. Miethe and Gary R. Habermas, *Why Believe? God Exists!* (Joplin: College Press, 1993). For specialized volumes on these and other important topics, see the bibliographies in these books.

9. See William Backus and Marie Chapian, *Telling Yourself the Truth* (Minneapolis: Bethany, 1980); William Backus, *The Good News about Worry* (Minneapolis: Bethany, 1991); Robert S. McGee, *The Search for Significance* (Houston: Rapha Publishing, 1987); Chris Thurman, *The Lies We Believe* (Nashville: Thomas Nelson, 1989).

10. Similar advice for replacing unbiblical thoughts with biblical truth is given in other texts. See the examples in Ps. 42:5-6,11; 43:5; Lam. 3:19-26; Rom. 1:25; 12:2; Jas. 4:7-10.

11. Backus and Chapian, *Telling Yourself the Truth*, Chapters 1–3, especially p. 15.

12. For details applied specifically to doubt, see Habermas, *The Thomas Factor*, where the chief focus of the entire volume is emotional uncertainty. See also Habermas, *Dealing with Doubt*, Chapter 4; Guinness, especially Chapter 10.

13. Again, this is no more than the briefest of comments on the subject and barely provides an idea of the direction one might follow. Important details are found in Habermas and Moreland, Chapter 15: "Becoming Heavenly Minded" and Habermas, *Dealing with Doubt*, Chapter 5.

SUGGESTED READINGS

Anderson, Lynn. *If I Really Believe, Why Do I Have These Doubts?* Minneapolis: Bethany, 1992.

Backus, William. *The Good News about Worry*. Minneapolis: Bethany, 1991.

Backus, William, and Marie Chapian. *Telling Yourself the Truth*. Minneapolis: Bethany, 1980.

Guinness, Os. *In Two Minds: The Dilemma of Doubt and How to Resolve It*. Downers Grove, IL: InterVarsity, 1976. Reissued as *Doubt*. Batavia, NY: Lion Publishing, 1987).

Habermas, Gary R. *Dealing with Doubt*. Chicago: Moody, 1990.

Habermas, Gary R. *The Thomas Factor: Using Your Doubts to Draw Closer to God*. Nashville: Broadman and Holman, 1999.

McGrath, Alister E. *The Sunnier Side of Doubt*. Grand Rapids: Zondervan, 1990.

Reflecting on Lesson Three

1. How would you give some specific counsel to either Kathy or Phillip? Did you notice any clues that provide some direction?

2. Do you agree that emotional doubt is the most common species, as well as the most painful? Why or why not?

3. Were you amazed at how often Jesus used His miracles, and His resurrection in particular, to confront doubt? What does this tell you?

4. Can you find any other examples of believers in Scripture who struggled with doubt? Why do you think it so common? What do you think that means?

5. For group discussion: What other misbeliefs do we tell ourselves about this subject? How many can you name? Do you agree that it is a widely misunderstood topic?

6. Group project: Practice counseling someone with doubts by having a volunteer make up a possible problem. Pick a counselor and do a mock session in front of the group. Take notes while this is going on. Compare your responses and answers with those that were given by the participants. What have you learned? Where could better replies have been given?

7. Talk to a believing friend who actually has doubts. See if, together, you can work through some of the relevant issues in his or her life.

8. For group discussion: Why is volitional doubt potentially so dangerous? How would you try to motivate someone who doesn't want to be motivated? Talk through several options.

Consider this:

Most adults, at least by their middle years, have suffered some form of painful loss or devastating trauma. The Bible is filled with stories and other texts which will help us through those times. If we have prepared our hearts with these passages before the trials come, we will be better able to cope when our lives are turned upside-down. Before reading Lesson Four consider Jesus' death, burial, and resurrection and what messages they provide to give us comfort in times of struggle. Ask yourself how your most painful experiences can be turned to bring glory to God.

4

GRIEF, SUFFERING, AND PAIN

In this lesson:

▶ The author's experience
▶ Grief over Lazarus's death
▶ Suffering in the light of eternity
▶ Persecution and the hope of resurrection
▶ Practicing a top-down perspective

___

I know firsthand the terrible sting of grief and pain. In 1995 my wife of 23 years passed away from cancer. She was only 43 years old. She was easily my best friend. Our four children still lived at home at the time. Next to losing her, my greatest concern was for my children. Because of their young ages, I felt like

I was suffering a double dose of grief — or worse. How would they recover? Would they have prolonged psychological scars? Would they blame the Lord? I simply didn't know the answers. I frequently said that this was the worst possible thing that could ever happen to me.

With my children, I simply let them set the pace for the issues that we discussed. I determined not to force any "lessons" on them unless they inquired about a topic. For myself, my most noticeable need was undoubtedly for the companionship I was missing. I was unspeakably thankful for the help I received from what I (unprejudicially!) consider to be the greatest family in the world. But after dealing with the day's situations, I still went up every night to an empty bed. How I missed her!

This time can best be summed up by another phrase I often used. It was my most common response when asked how we were doing. "The Lord is good," I answered. The ways I could see His hand in our lives were just too numerous to mention. Our family traveled just one day at a time. My mother would often comment, "God is leading us ever so gently." It became the trademark of our conversations. In spite of our enormous grief and pain, it was always bearable.

We learned so many lessons along the way, too. At times I even discovered that I was monitoring myself. Having written a volume on death and the afterlife just three years before she died (dedicated to Debbie!),[1] I was observing my reactions, in comparison to the classic signs of grief. Then, two years after her death, I wrote another book, almost as a diary on grief, including my family's struggles and our triumphs.[2]

What does Christianity in general, and the resurrection of Jesus in particular, have to say to those who grieve? Is our advice significantly different from what non-Christians might offer? Is

our perspective any different? And does anything
ever touch the tremen-
dous pain of loss, or the
other suffering we en-
counter in life? The sub-

What does Christianity with
its resurrection gospel have
to say to those who grieve?

title of the book about my wife's sickness presents my angle: it
was, indeed, "a personal account of grief and resurrection." The
last word, in particular, puts all the rest in perspective.

GRIEF

How did Jesus handle the experience of grief? What did He do
after the death of his close friend, Lazarus, whom He loved (John
11:3,5)? Unquestionably, Jesus was affected. John tells us that he
was troubled. Then, in the shortest verse in the Bible, "Jesus
wept" (vv. 33,35). To those watching, it was obvious that Jesus
loved His friend (v. 36). He felt the pain of others, too, even
when He knew He would raise His friend from the dead!

Jesus spent some time counseling especially with Martha,
Lazarus's sister, when He arrived in Bethany. She and her sister
Mary were being comforted by a number of Jews. Martha came
out to meet Him (vv. 17-20).

Martha began by voicing her anguish. Surely, if Jesus had
come just a little sooner, Lazarus would not have died (v. 21).
There seems to be a hint of disapproval here. If so, it is difficult
to know why, since Lazarus had died before Jesus could have
arrived (cf. vv. 6,17). This is the voice of grief — it doesn't always
place frustration in the right spot. Still, Martha was greatly
relieved to see Jesus. He was certainly a strong individual whose
words and presence would offer great comfort during this stren-

uous time. He had power with God (v. 22). However, it doesn't seem that Martha hoped He could raise her brother, since, just moments later, she thought that his resurrection would only occur in the last days (v. 24). Then, when they went to the tomb, she was not sure removing the stone was a good idea because of the odor (v. 39).

Jesus responded by reminding her that Lazarus would be raised from the dead (v. 23). Reciting good Jewish theology, Martha understood only the future ramifications of this doctrine — of course her brother would rise again with all of the other righteous dead (v. 24). But Jesus explained that there was also a present benefit to this doctrine that she was apparently not taking into account. Jesus *Himself* is both the resurrection and life. Those who believe in Him will live, even if they die. In fact, they will never die (vv. 25-26). As

> Jesus *Himself* is both the resurrection and life.

Jesus would explain briefly to the believing thief on the cross next to Him (Luke 23:43), consciousness does not cease at death.

This is a tremendous truth that we ought not miss, for it has great application to the struggles of life. Greek scholar A.T. Robertson expressed Jesus' teaching like this: "This reply was startling enough. They are not mere doctrines about future events, but present realities in Jesus Himself . . . . here he means more, even that Lazarus is now alive." Then our Lord goes on in verse 26 to apply the truth to others. No one who lives while believing in Jesus will ever die. Robertson comments that John chose a strong double negative to express this truth: believers "'shall not die for ever' (eternal death)."[3] While Lazarus may have died, or fallen asleep as Jesus says (11:11), there is no eternal death here. He is both alive at present and will be raised in the future, in a new body.[4]

Jesus then asked Martha if she believed this. It was exam time. Jesus wondered if she could apply what she believed. His friend responded positively, affirming her faith in Him as the Messiah, the Son of God (v. 27). Here, then, was the main issue. Just like so many of us today, Martha didn't make the connection between her belief and her life, including her feelings. If Jesus was truly the Son of God, then He was the Lord of life, just as He was explaining to her. He both ensured the future and could raise her brother in the present, if He desired. If He didn't, the fact remained that Lazarus was even then living.

Jesus' words must have made an impression on her, for she broke off the conversation at that point and went to get her sister Mary (v. 28), probably so she could hear these encouraging teachings, too. But Martha certainly didn't understand the full impact of Jesus' words. Verse 39 shows that she still was not expecting Lazarus to be raised from the dead. Then Jesus reminded her of His statements to her — He was, indeed, the Lord of life (v. 40).

When Mary arrived, she expressed the same opinion her sister did. Lazarus wouldn't have died if Jesus had come earlier (v. 32). They had probably said this among themselves. Perhaps the sisters didn't know that Jesus had received the message too late. Jesus was moved by the grief of Mary and those who were comforting her (v. 33-36). He responded by raising Lazarus from the dead (vv. 38-45), which He had planned to do from the outset (vv. 4-6,11,14-16).

Jesus approached Mary and Martha as He would do later with His disciples. He confronted grief, first and foremost, by presenting both the facts and their meanings. He emphasized the full impact of believing relevant truth. His own resurrection was the chief answer for His disciples, just as Lazarus's raising would be for the sisters and those with them.[5]

But before He performed the miracle, He instructed Martha once again on the meaning of resurrection, since there were several things she still did not realize (v. 40). Her theology did not allow for her brother to live before the last day. But Jesus taught her that Lazarus did not cease to exist before the final raising of his body. Further, she had forgotten the true meaning of the Deity and power of Jesus. He could raise her brother. She failed to apply her theology to her emotional struggles. Her beliefs remained separated from her practical spirituality.

In both the cases of the disciples and with Lazarus' sisters, the truth of life after death was the foundation for Jesus' comments. Jesus confronted both grief and erroneous doctrine with facts and correct teaching. We learn not only that counseling those who are grieving is important, but we may begin to formulate our own strategy for dealing with contemporary cases.

> Jesus confronted both grief and erroneous doctrine with facts and correct teaching.

SUFFERING

This is a subject that is frequently addressed in Scripture. What part does Jesus' resurrection play in other sorts of suffering that Christians experience? Do we discover any advice that can be applied to our lives, especially during the times of pain?

Paul entertains the question of suffering in 2 Corinthians 4:7-18. The apostle begins by talking about how often he had been exposed to death. Problems and persecutions of various sorts had made him very much aware that his body was fragile, like a clay jar that could easily be smashed (vv. 7-12). This text is somewhat reminiscent of 2 Corinthians 11:24-32, where Paul gives a long list of painful persecutions and other hurts from his life.

In both passages, he directs the praise to God — the One who raised Jesus from the dead and will raise believers, too (4:14). For Paul, the resurrection was the event that made suffering worthwhile. It is what ensures our eternal destinies. So Paul never quit, or lost his motivation. Though his physical body was declining, his "inner nature" was being rejuvenated (v. 16).

Paul reaches a splendid crescendo in the last two verses of this chapter. Because of these truths, he tells believers to redirect their thinking:

> For our light and momentary troubles are achieving for us an eternal glory that far outweighs them all. So we fix our eyes not on what is seen, but on what is unseen. For what is seen is temporary, but what is unseen is eternal (vv. 17-18).

In these glorious words, Paul explains that the believer's sufferings are worth it all. Coming from someone who endured what he did, this is quite a confession! We can learn from someone who paid this kind of price. And he testified that our problems gain eternal treasures that make the tough times on earth far more than worth it all. Because of this reality, Christians should not focus on life's dilemmas. Our concentration should be fixed on eternity. Its blessings should motivate us to heavenly action.

A very similar theme is sounded in Romans 8. The Spirit who raised Jesus Christ from the dead will also raise believers (v. 11). Therefore, we should live by the Spirit and not give in to the desires of our sin natures, for we are God's children and fellow-heirs with Jesus. By sharing His sufferings, we will also share His glory (vv. 12-

17)! Accordingly, "I consider that our present sufferings are not worth comparing with the glory that will be revealed in us" (v. 18).

In both of these passages, the resurrection of Jesus guarantees that the

> The resurrection of Jesus guarantees that the believer will be raised, too.

believer will be raised, too. Our suffering, then, is to be considered in light of eternity. From that exalted perspective, several things are viewed more clearly: we can see our problems for what they are, temporal situations. Further, these issues give us occasion to deepen our Christian character, as we use the Lord's power to avoid sin. In so doing, suffering increases our heavenly treasures. In sum, this is why we are to meditate on eternity, our heavenly home. It not only provides assurance concerning our future, but it pays dividends in the present, as well.

PERSECUTION

The persecution of Christians was a very real possibility while the New Testament was being written. Though not as widespread as it would become a couple of hundred years later, these were still tough times. A husband, wife, or child could be separated from their families at a moment's notice. In some areas, there was always the potential that every day at home could be the last one. More than one New Testament book reflects this situation and Jesus' resurrection was often used as the stimulus for hope.

The Book of Revelation gives constant encouragement to those who suffer for their faith. The messages are delivered by Jesus, the first to be raised from the dead (1:2,4-5). Exalted and glorified, He appears in the very first chapter as the One who was dead, but is now the Living One, who would never die again. He holds the keys to death and Hades (1:17-18).

From the outset, then, the Giver of the revelation in this book is the One who has already experienced the worst that men could do. He paid the ultimate penalty for obeying His Father's will. He is the One who was pierced (1:7). But now He is triumphant over death and the wicked dead, controlling the keys that determine who spends eternity separated from Him.

This is quite an introduction! Who could better sympathize with believers who are suffering for His Name? And who would Christians more want on their side than the Righteous Judge who determines where each of us spends eternity?

So when He encourages those in Smyrna not to be afraid for the things they are about to suffer, including imprisonment and other injustices, it is meaningful that the speaker is the One who died and returned to life again. It is all the more profound when it is the risen Lord who said that some of them may even be called upon

> Only after personally walking the path of persecution and death does Jesus encourage believers to be faithful in doing the same.

to die for their faith. Those will receive the crown of life (2:8-10). Jesus Christ identified with their troubles. He is not a detached being who removes Himself from the human plight. Only after personally walking the path of persecution and death does He encourage them to be faithful in doing the same.

Jesus appears again in chapter 5 as a sacrificial Lamb who was now alive. In the next chapter, martyred saints cry out to the living Lamb for retribution against their slayers, and they are told that they will first be joined by other Christians who will also die

for their faith (5:9-11). Later, we are told that martyred saints over-
came Satan by the blood of the Lamb and their testimony, since
they loved the Lord more than their own lives (12:10-11). This is
reminiscent of Jesus' teachings. By losing their lives, believers
gained eternal life (John 12:25).

So Revelation links the risen Jesus with suffering for the
gospel. Allison Trites sums it up very nicely:

> The testimony of Christians in the Apocalypse of John is
> predicated on the resurrection of Christ. Without his personal
> conquest of the grave, there would be no message of hope
> and no inspiration for martyrs to give their lives . . . . It was of
> the utmost practical importance for John to remind suffering
> Christians that Jesus Christ had conquered death, and that
> therefore they could expect to share in his eternal victory over
> sin and death if they remained faithful.[6]

The Book of Hebrews is also directed to persecuted believers,
as indicated in some key passages.[7] It is somewhat surprising that
the resurrection of Jesus is mentioned directly in only one text
(13:20-21). However, William Lane points out that the entire
emphasis of this book is on Jesus' sacrificial death and His exaltation to heaven. But the former requires the resurrection for its
meaning and the latter "serves as an inclusive reference to Jesus'
resurrection, ascension, and continuing reign" (cf. 1:3; 7:16,24-25).[8]
Jesus' resurrection, then, is an intricate part of the message for
persecuted Christians in Hebrews to remain true to their faith.

Peter provides the clearest passage linking the resurrection of
Jesus with persecution (1 Pet. 1:3-9). The apostle begins by
explaining that believers have a new hope in the Lord Jesus
Christ. His resurrection from the dead has secured blessings for
us in heaven, an inheritance that "can never perish, spoil or
fade" (1 Pet. 1:4). These blessings are indestructible (*aphtharton*

— a form of the term "immortal"), and without any blemish (*amianton*) or loss of glory (*amaranton*). They are "reserved" (*teteremenen*), guarded for us by the power of God Himself. They will neither be taken away nor corrupted. Our eternal inheritance is securely kept for us by the grace and power of God.

Peter then draws a wonderful conclusion from all of this. Because of this heavenly hope, believers should triumph even during their trials (v. 6), most likely a reference to the persecution discussed in 1 Peter 4:12-19. The word "rejoice" (*agalliasthe*) is a strong term referring to exuberant joy in the face of their suffering! Giving the exhortation even more meaning is that Peter was no stranger to persecution. Jesus had predicted Peter's martyrdom (John 21:18-19) and, just a few decades later, Clement listed Peter and Paul as "champions" and "noble examples" for believers, in that they were persecuted unto death, all the time remaining faithful to their Lord.[9]

So why does Peter command believers to rejoice during persecution? He states in the first words of verse six that the reason for celebrating is based on the truths of the previous three verses. So Peter's message to Christians centers on the fact of Jesus' resurrection and the glories of heaven that are secured through it. This present anticipation of future blessings should bring us comfort, regardless of the circumstances around us. If we could only bring ourselves to do a better job of applying the lesson that Peter had learned through his own trials!

CAN IT MAKE A PRACTICAL DIFFERENCE IN THIS LIFE?

Grief, pain, suffering, and persecution are tough subjects. If the Christian could somehow bring God's truth to bear on the hurts of life, this would surely be an added benefit of faith. Is it possible to *really* be changed by the New Testament message?

In the last chapter, we outlined Paul's method in Philippians 4:6-9 for dealing with anxiety. There he presented four steps to be applied to our worries. Interestingly, Paul's word in verse seven for the peace of God that will *guard* our hearts is the same term that Peter chose in 1 Peter 1:5 for Christians being protected by God's power (*phroureo*). Apparently, both apostles thought that these could be literal realities in the Christian's life, rather than theoretical possibilities alone.

In this chapter, we have seen that Jesus, Paul, John, Hebrews, and Peter all agree that Jesus' resurrection is the key to victory. Precisely because Jesus was raised, believers will be raised, and eternal life in heaven is secure. Therefore, each one said that we should focus our attention not on present problems, but on the significance of future realities. In volume I, we called this the "top-down" perspective on the issues of life. We will not repeat those thoughts here, but this is what the New Testament means by living above our daily struggles.

> The key is to *practice* replacing our present perspective with heavenly truth until it becomes a habit.

On many occasions, I have seen this outlook totally transform a person's life. The key is to *practice* replacing our present perspective with heavenly truth until it becomes a habit, just like Paul states in Philippians 4:8-9. It doesn't happen overnight. But each time we substitute God's teaching in place of an earthly concern, we gain momentum and strength. When we fail, we need to pick ourselves up and start again. Each success will bring us a step closer to our goal of peace.

Really, it's quite simply done. We just have to practice. We must stop telling ourselves fearful things like "I'm going to flunk that exam tomorrow," or "What if I lose my job?" picturing all the horrible problems. Instead, we can forcefully substitute other, more wholesome thoughts: "What difference will this situation make 100 years from now?" "It probably won't even bother me next week!" Even better, we need to remind ourselves of "higher" truth: "Our worth is definitely *not* caught up in what we *do* but in who God says we *are*. If we are in Christ, having eternal life with God and our believing loved ones, what more must we have here?" "He didn't even spare His own Son for us" (Rom. 8:32)! "We will actually share Christ's glory as joint heirs" (8:17)! "Other things might be nice, but I don't *have* to have *any* of them."

Concerning pain and suffering, a heavenly perspective on our hurts tells us that everything will ultimately be just fine. God will either heal us here or in heaven, and maybe both! Jesus taught us not to be afraid of those who can only take our lives, but to fear God, who determines our eternal futures (Matt. 10:28). True, no one wants to lose their life. But the point, once again, is one of perspective. *Even if* that happens, we have eternal life.

This is also Paul's message. Immediately after the major passage that we discussed above, he said that, if we die, we will have a new resurrection body and an eternal home in heaven (2 Cor. 5:1). He longs for that time (v. 2). Even at death, he also knows that leaving the body means that we will be with Christ (v. 8).

In another wonderfully comforting text, Paul also teaches the top-down outlook on death. He declares that dying is actually gain (Phil. 1:21)! Do we believe that? In case we missed his point, two verses later he tells us that he longs to die and be with Christ because *this is better by far* (v. 23). Yet, this was not inconsistent with his also being pleased to continue his ministry if, in so doing, he could assist others (vv. 24-25). We need to work through each of these points as well as many related ones, repeating them forcefully as often as they are needed.

But how can this start helping us today? Many scholars agree that emotional anguish is worse (perhaps even *far* worse) than physical suffering. I've heard people say that if they could get rid of their chronic anxiety or depression they would *literally* give their arm. The top-down perspective tells us that we *can* eliminate

> Do we believe Paul when he declares that dying is gain?

the type of pain that we add to our problems by the way we think. Continually asking ourselves, "But what if it gets worse?" or feeding our anger, lack of forgiveness, or self-hatred, all cause terrible pain. Even if we're not dominated by anxiety or depression, we still add daily pain to ourselves by the things we tell ourselves — the exact opposite of thinking God's thoughts as in Philippians 4:8.

I have a long way to go, but when I first began applying top-down thinking, I was simply amazed at the *large amounts* of pain I had added to my life. But I didn't realize how much it was until some of it actually began to subside. Then, I could more clearly see *how much more there was that I hadn't cleaned out yet!* Leaving this emotional and mental suffering behind is nothing short of life-changing. It simplifies our lives by teaching us what is worth concentrating on. It keeps us from being so fragmented that we cannot enjoy the ride.

But, with God's help, we need to be tenacious about it! We have to start with the desire to apply these teachings. The stronger we are about *actually doing it*, the faster it will work. Don't be deceived here — it really does work. But, of course, nothing will happen if we don't apply God's standards, like those in Philippians 4:6-9. Like Paul ends the subject in verse nine, we must practice these things until they become a part of us.

APPLICATION

This topic is just loaded with possibilities for application to our lives. In fact, the entire last section is one that needs to be considered as part of our practice. We will begin with a brief conclusion from those thoughts.

First, the top-down outlook on life promises *both* an eternal home with God and others, *and* relief from some (or even much) of our suffering, beginning right now. Could anything be better than that? It's there for the application. As they say, the choice is ours.

Perhaps an illustration would help. How many times have we gone to the doctor's office, secretly wondering

> The top-down outlook on life promises *both* an eternal home *and* relief from some suffering right now.

(but embarrassed to say it out loud!) if this could be something life threatening? The longer and more ardently we've worried about it, the more the pain is relieved when we are told that it is only the flu. Have you ever felt a huge tide of positive emotion wash over you after the diagnosis? "The flu? That's nothing. I can take that!" we tell ourselves. Then we take a deep breath. We feel like we could conquer the world.

The pain that just subsided is an actual example of just some of what we bring upon ourselves *simply by thinking the wrong way about something!* Like Martha, we might know good theology, but we cause ourselves distress by not living it. That suffering is precisely what can be eliminated if we change our thinking to a heavenly vantage point. Then there is the eternal life as a nice extra blessing!

Second, Jesus' talk with Martha provides special ammunition for grieving believers. Williams translates John 11:25-26 this way:

"Jesus said to her, 'I am the resurrection and the life myself. Whoever continues to believe in me will live right on, even though he dies, and no person who continues to live and believe in me will ever die at all. Do you believe this?'"[10]

One other consideration of Martha's and Mary's grief is this. Their pain was not because their brother was not presently alive, but beacuse they missed him. And Jesus plainly missed Lazarus, too. But, as Paul tells us, there is much difference between grieving *with* hope for the future, and grieving *without* hope (1 Thess 4:13). For Christians, we have the knowledge that we will see our loved ones again, all because of Jesus' resurrection (4:14).

> Resurrection is not just a future *aspect* of life — it *is* life.

The passage in John 11 shows that resurrection is not just a future *aspect* of life — it *is* life. True, we do not have our resurrection bodies and we have not seen heaven. But, Christians have already received the first dividends on our heavenly bank accounts. While we are still in this world, eternal life has been given as the gift of God's grace. We have it now (John 5:24; 6:47), and we can know that we have it in the future (1 John 5:13). Further, it even affects the present, as in our discussion of how it can quiet much of our emotional pain. It streamlines our lives if we will allow it, making us single-minded in our pursuit of God. And by living simply, we also keep more pain from entering, due to having changed our faulty thinking.

Third, some have noted that we may have an interesting hint of Jesus' mind-set from the word "groaned" (*enebrimesato*), which John uses twice in John 11:33,38. The term in the New Testament shows anger or indignation. If this is the way John meant it, the question would be, what made Jesus upset? The second time (v. 38), it could have been because His power was questioned in the previous verse.

But this wouldn't explain at least the earlier use of the term. Even though the women had made some mild objections, these were hardly out of place, given the death of their brother. It has been said that what displeased Jesus could well have been the realities of sin and death. Thus, standing before His good friend's tomb, He was forcefully reminded of the hold that these twin evils have on the human life — including His own. He hurt, too.

The cross especially shows the love of God. He loved us before we loved Him (1 John 4:10,19). He even loved us while we were still unlovely (Rom. 5:8). And He loved us enough to let His Son suffer and die in order to bless us (Rom. 8:32). In short, the cross proves that God both understands suffering and that He loved each of us enough to go to that extent in spite of the pain. We might say that we don't know why we suffer, but we shouldn't question His goodness.

Fourth, this leads us to another topic that we will just mention here, since it is the subject of a future discussion. Death anxiety is an ill of its own. We are told that Jesus came in order to release us from slavery to the fear of death, which holds us in bondage throughout our lives (Heb. 2:14-15). Producing its own brand of pain, we want to see what angle Jesus' resurrection brings to this subject, too. But we will devote an entire chapter to this issue.

NOTES

1. Co-authored with J.P. Moreland, *Immortality: The Other Side of Death* (Nashville: Thomas Nelson, 1992).

2. For a description of our family's pilgrimage and many of these lessons, see Gary R. Habermas, *Forever Loved: A Personal Account of Grief and Resurrection* (Joplin, MO: College Press, 1997).

3. A.T. Robertson, *Word Pictures in the New Testament* (Nashville: Broadman Press, 1932), Volume V, pp. 199-200.

4. Both present and future aspects are also clearly seen in Jesus' teaching in John 5:24-25.

5. This is reminiscent of Jesus' answer to John the Baptist's doubt, where His miracles also played a key role. Jesus' raising of the dead served an important function there, too (Luke 7:22).

6. Allison Trites, "Witness and the Resurrection in the Apocalypse of John," in *Life in the Face of Death: The Resurrection Message of the New Testament,* ed. by Richard N. Longenecker (Grand Rapids: Eerdmans, 1998), p. 281.

7. See Hebrews 10:32-35; 11:35-38 followed by 12:2-4.

8. William L. Lane, "Living a Life of Faith in the Face of Death: The Witness of Hebrews," in *Life in the Face of Death*, pp. 264–266.

9. Clement, Corinthians 5. For the text here, see *The Apostolic Fathers*, tr. and ed. by J.B. Lightfoot (Grand Rapids: Baker, 1891, reprint, 1971).

10. John 11:25-26 in Charles B. Williams, *The New Testament in the Language of the People* (Chicago: Moody, 1966).

SUGGESTED READINGS

Green, Michael. *The Empty Cross of Jesus.* Downers Grove, IL: InterVarsity, 1984. Chapter 13.

Lane, William L. "Living a Life of Faith in the Face of Death: The Witness of Hebrews." In *Life in the Face of Death: The Resurrection Message of the New Testament.* Ed. by Richard N. Longenecker. Grand Rapids: Eerdmans, 1998.

Lewis, C.S. *The Problem of Pain.* New York: Macmillan, 1962.

Trites, Allison. "Witness and the Resurrection in the Apocalypse of John." In *Life in the Face of Death: The Resurrection Message of the New Testament.* Ed. by Richard N. Longenecker Grand Rapids: Eerdmans, 1998.

Reflecting on Lesson Four

1. What are some areas where, like Martha, you do not live what your theology tells you is true? List some examples. Why do we so often fail to think in terms of what we believe?

2. For group discussion: Why do you think that we, also like Martha, so frequently tell ourselves things that only hurt us worse? Do you think we are usually aware of our false beliefs, or not? Support your answers.

3. Do you think that Jesus expressed indignation in John 11:33,38? If so, what do you think the reason was?

4. Besides those that we listed above, can you name any other benefits of our present possession and knowledge of eternal life?

5. In what other ways does the cross of Jesus reveal God's love for us, as well as His understanding of our pain? Write down a few specific examples, along with a paragraph explanation of each one.

6. For group discussion: Besides relieving some of our emotional pain, what other practical benefits do you think we gain from applying the "top-down" principle to our lives?

Consider this:

By now you have a clear understanding of what is meant by the "top-down" perspective on life. In preparation for Lesson Five, consider how this "top-down" perspective would provide the power to overcome sin.

5

DAILY POWER AND PRAISE

In this lesson:

▶ Power against sin
▶ The internal nature of sin
▶ Christ our high priest
▶ Putting the power to work in our lives

How do you handle the temptation to sin? Although he was known in his church as a strong leader, Justin struggled mightily with a private sin: his enslavement to pornography. It almost seemed that, when the opportunity presented itself, his feet just naturally moved in that direction. No matter how much he thought, "No, no, no . . ." to himself, there he was, where he knew he shouldn't be. Yet, he also knew he wouldn't have made the decision to indulge unless that was his stronger desire. The last thought bothered him.

How could he break this habit that he despised so much? He noticed its affects in his views toward his wife and children. But those thoughts scared him even more. He talked with a couple of very close friends whom he trusted. He studied Scripture, especially the subjects of God's condemnation of sexual sins. He told himself repeatedly what a loser he was. Sometimes it worked and he seemed to avoid the situations. Many times it didn't work. He grew even more frustrated. "Sometimes I just don't care any more," he lied to himself.

He found no substantial relief until he changed his direction. He began weekly meetings with a wise Christian friend. Together they studied the nature of sin, discovering some incredible truths that changed how he viewed the subject. Then they did some careful thinking about the subject of motivation. Justin started realizing that sin was best avoided because he loved something else more, and not as much because he hated what he was doing.

> Sin is best avoided when we love something else more.

This translated into some specific actions. When faced with the normal temptations, he began to ask himself some questions. Slowly he began to make some progress. Occasional setbacks served as the impetus to start again, with a renewed zeal. Along the way, he learned a new recipe for pursuing spirituality, too. We will describe the lessons he learned and what brought the eventual victory as we continue through this chapter.

RESURRECTION POWER

One of the most obvious aspects of Jesus' resurrection was the awesome power involved. In the New Testament accounts, we catch glimpses of the authority, might, and knowledge that were required by such an act. The resurrection invoked not only the mighty power of creation itself, but a species of creative agency that had never before been manifested in the world. In a very special sense, the resurrection signalled the inbreaking of God's new creation. It was a demonstration not only of His omnipotence and omniscience in relation to Jesus' glorious new body, but also of His personal involvement with our deepest needs. In its very essence, Jesus' resurrection was even a fore-taste of the new life of heaven, a harbinger of the coming age of God's eternal Kingdom.

It is just incredible that Paul notes more than once that the majestic power of God manifested in Jesus' resurrection is avail-able to the believer in this present life! The result is that this power can transform us. In particular, it can even allow the obedient believer to overcome sin so that it no longer characterizes his daily life. We're not talking about being perfect, but about the possibil-ity of living a life that is characterized by making good choices.

In one of his most pointed statements on the subject, Paul declared in Philippians 3:10 that it was his desire to know the power of Jesus Christ's resurrection from the dead. The word Paul uses here for "power" (*dunamin*) is the word from which we get English words like "dynamo." This same word in the New Testament is often used to speak of God's might, the perform-ance of miracles, or the power of angels.[1] Paul wants the strength to overcome sin and grow in his Christian life. From this and related passages, he desired to both know and apply God's power in his own life.

For instance, in Ephesians 1:18-21 Paul prayed that, among other blessings, believers might come to know the "incomparably great power" available to them. Providing more details, Paul states that this power is from God Himself, the same might that raised Jesus Christ from the dead and exalted Him above all (vv. 19–21).

To understand that the *same* power that raised Jesus is also available to *me* is both mind-boggling and humbling at the same time. No wonder Paul wanted to experience that same power in his own life! Paul also prays that God would strengthen believers with His power through the work of the Holy Spirit in their lives (Eph. 3:16-17). This power can bring us into a deeper relationship with God (3:19).

OVERCOMING SIN

How can we be more specific with regard to God's resurrection power being available to Christians? Does Paul provide details concerning how this power may be used in the believer's life? How can we tap into it?

> The *same* power that raised Jesus is also available to *me*.

Continuing his idea that it is the power of Jesus' resurrection that is available to us, Paul draws an illustration regarding baptism in Romans 6:4-14.[2] He points out by analogy that believers were buried with Jesus in baptism in order to signify our participation in His death. Being raised out of the water indicates our being raised from the dead with Him, signifying a new life. As a result, Christians are united with Christ, both in His death and in His resurrection (vv. 4-5).

Taking the analogy further, we are told that our old sin nature was crucified with Jesus, so we are freed from sin (vv. 6-7,9). As a result, believers should regard themselves as being dead to sin but alive to God (v. 11). The conclusion of the entire matter, then, is that the Christian should shun sin and offer himself for God's service (vv. 12-14).

In a similar passage (Col. 2:11-14), Paul makes use of the same analogy of being buried with Jesus in His baptism, hence forsaking our sinful desires, only to be raised from the dead with Him, making us alive to God. It is "faith in the power of God" that brings all of this about (v. 12). Once again, the power of God manifested in the resurrection of Jesus accounts for the Christian's deliverance from sin. We have a new orientation towards God.

Further development of these ideas occurs in Romans 8:9-11. Believers can actually be controlled, not by their sinful passions, but by the Holy Spirit. The resurrection of Jesus is still a focus here. The same God who raised Jesus has now given us His Spirit.

The same God who raised Jesus has now given His Spirit to live in us and completely change us. So the power of God in the Person of the Holy Spirit now works in the believer's life.

Perhaps a good summary statement of this entire subject is found in Paul's words in Galatians 2:20. His point appears to be that his mortal, sinful body died on the cross with Jesus precisely so that he no longer needed to live for himself. Rather, Christ now lived through him and was the Agent for the change in his life by virtue of His own power.

THE NATURE OF SIN

I am convinced that part of the reason we fall prey to sin is that we have a wrong view of what it is, as well as underestimating its power. We look in the wrong place, concluding that our enemy is nowhere to be seen. The end result is that we lose many battles to temptation.

The Pharisees in the Gospels seemed to view sin like dirt. For example, they criticized Jesus' disciples because they failed to wash their hands before eating (Matt. 15:1-2). Many believers seem to agree with this view. We frequently don't go certain places and don't do certain things, because sin may rub off on us — sort of like an infectious disease. Therefore, it is something outside us, and we dare not allow it to make its way inside us.

This is one of those subjects where a half-truth can be worse than a lie. Jesus responded to the Pharisees that the sin that corrupts us comes from within — from our heart. Murder, immorality, lying, and stealing all come from inside us, not from external sources like eating with dirty hands (Matt. 15:18-20). We produce good and bad speech and actions from within ourselves, according to what is in us (Matt. 12:33-37). Sin has its birth in our thought life (Matt. 5:27).

James similarly tells us that our temptations come from within. Sin results from being enticed by our own desires, which gives birth to evil (Jas. 1:14-16). So the battle is an internal one. Murder, coveting, and fighting originate in us, leading to the acts themselves (Jas. 4:1-3). We need to repent of this sin (4:8-10).

But not only is sin an internal problem, coming from our own ungodly desires, but there is another problem. And this one may even be worse. The view that sin is primarily external in nature also leads to other faulty positions — that, again like dirt, it can be quickly washed off with little or no ill affect. Thus, a quick confession removes all of the harm of sin. We might even be tempted to argue that a little guilt is a fair trade for enjoying a brief indulgence in sin.

These errors may be worse than the first. To underestimate the addictiveness and hardening qualities of sin are among the worst mistakes of all. Throughout Scripture, we learn that a little sin frequently leads to much more. It is usually easier to repeat a sin or to perform another once the barrier is broken. But the scariest truth of all is that sin hardens our hearts. It slowly, almost imperceptibly, can replace our first love. Our motivation to follow the Lord may be supplanted by lesser, more base desires.

> To underestimate the addictiveness and hardening qualities of sin are among the worst mistakes of all.

The author of Hebrews, for example, draws a parallel between the Israelites, who willfully sinned and hardened their hearts against the Lord (Heb. 3:7-11), and Christians who choose to disobey the Lord (3:12-15). Sinning is deceitful (v. 13) — it is cunning, sly, misleading, and devious. It is definitely a tricky matter. Worse, it can trick us — hardening our hearts in unbelief (v. 13). It can lead to a state where we are not interested in God.

Sinning can overcome us little by little. The change may even be imperceptible, at least in the beginning. What's worse, the affected person often does not recognize the change at all, wrongly thinking that they are the same as before. But the end result is to actually side with the evil desires against God. The term "unbelief" (*apistias*) is a refusal to believe; it is an active state rather than simply a passive condition (v. 12). So the author exhorts us to be alert and take heed of these possibilities (v. 12). Sin blunts our motivation to follow God. We are to continue encouraging each other to avoid these painful consequences (v. 13).

So the picture we get here is quite different from the one with which we began. Sin comes from our hearts, from the inside out. This does not mean that outside influences cannot affect us, only that such influences must be allowed into our thought processes and germinated there. The internal result and the external action make us unclean. We often cultivate the sin so that it grows to maturity. It can overcome us little by little. It can even cause us to turn against God.[3]

Justin learned some of these things during his own study with his friend. They concluded that sin was an internal problem of the will that got a stronger grip on us the more we indulged in it. He realized that he needed a different motivation, concluding that positive reinforcement was more powerful than the more legalistic stance he sometimes tended to take.

But we would be mistaken to imply that Paul's exhortation for believers to employ the power of the resurrection only applies to conquering sin in our lives. While this is a chief emphasis in the passages we mentioned, it is not his entire message. In the Application section below, we will address the crucial question of how we can be more successful in using this power to live above temptations to sin, as well as living the Christian life.

OUR EXALTED HIGH PRIEST

Before dealing with how victory over sin might be a daily reality in the believer's life, a related question should also be posed. How is Jesus involved in our daily lives? More particularly, what part does He actually play in our striving to conquer sin?

We have seen that the power for changing our sinful tendencies comes from the Lord Himself. Further, He has given us the Holy Spirit in order to effect the necessary guidance. So the Source and the power for victory are beyond the believer's own abilities.

Another provision in the battle against sin comes from the Scripture. This is another legacy of the Risen Lord, who had earlier promised the Holy Spirit's inspiration (see John 14:25-26; 15:26-27; 16:12-15). In a sense, the New Testament is the collection of love letters provided for us by the Lord.

In addition to the availability of God's power, the presence of the Holy Spirit, and the Scriptures, Jesus continues to take an active role in the lives of Christians today. Not only did He pray for future believers before He returned to His heaven (John 17:20), but He continues at present to intercede for them before His Father (Heb. 7:25).

> Jesus continues to take an active role in the lives of Christians today.

After Jesus' resurrection He appeared to His disciples, speaking about the Kingdom of God for forty days, after which He returned to His Father (Acts 1:1-11). The ascension was an important part of the early church preaching, for it signaled both Jesus' exaltation to heaven at God's right hand and the sending of the Holy Spirit (Acts 2:32-33; 5:30-32).

Paul sums it up nicely by citing an early Christian confession in 1 Timothy 3:16 which states that after His public ministry, Jesus "was taken up in glory." This must have been an especially meaningful truth for Paul, for a few years after His ascension it was in His glory that Jesus appeared to him.

So the resurrection event began the process that led to Jesus' appearances, ascension, glorification, and exaltation, as well as in His continuing position as our High Priest. The writer of Hebrews explains that His priesthood is a permanent one, since Jesus was raised from the dead and lives forever. Thus He is able not only to save us, but also to continually intercede for us before the Father (Heb. 7:23-25; 13:20; cf. 1 Tim. 2:5).

Paul further explains the significance of this doctrine. That the risen Jesus is constantly interceding for us is part of the reason which ensures that Christians will never be separated from the saving love of Jesus (Rom. 8:34-39). It is another aspect of the believer's arsenal in the daily struggle against sin (cf. 8:33).

> He is able not only to save us, but also to continually intercede for us before the Father.

So Jesus did not leave believers to find their own way in the world, either in the first century or in the twenty-first. He gave us plenty of weapons (2 Cor. 10:4). He promised that His apostles would be inspired by the Holy Spirit, resulting decades later in the completed New Testament. Before that was accomplished, He sent the Holy Spirit to believers, giving them the power to live a holy life. Following Jesus' death, resurrection, and ascension, He was exalted to His position of High Priest and Mediator on behalf of Christians. He now intercedes for us and assists us in our strivings to conquer sin. His provisions assist us to live for Him.

PRAISE AND WORSHIP

The resurrected Jesus, both before and after His exaltation to His Father's right hand, received praise and worship from His followers. It began at His very first appearance. On their way back from the empty tomb, the women saw Jesus, held Him by the feet and worshiped Him (Matt. 28:9). Later, after Mary Magdalene's return to the tomb, she also held on to Him and wouldn't let Him go (John 20:17)![4] While worship is not mentioned, this is the most likely meaning of her actions.

One week later, Jesus appeared to Thomas after he refused to believe. When the skeptical apostle saw Him, he exclaimed, "My

Lord and my God" (John 20:28). By the use of this latter title, Thomas had given Jesus the highest possible praise in the universe.[5] In a later appearance on a Galilean mountainside, those who saw Jesus again worshiped Him (Matt. 28:17). After His ascension to heaven, the disciples frequented the temple, continually praising God (Luke 24:51-52).

In one of the greatest passages in Scripture, Paul worships His exalted and glorified Lord. He tells us that Jesus Christ, who had God's nature, took on the nature of man. Submitting Himself in humility and obedience, He died on the cross (Phil. 2:6-8). Then Paul goes on:

> Therefore God exalted him to the highest place
> and gave him the name that is above every name,
> that at the name of Jesus every knee should bow,
> in heaven and on earth and under the earth,
> and every tongue confess that Jesus Christ is Lord,
> to the glory of God the Father (Phil. 2:9-11).

In this glorious hymn of praise, we are told that the risen and exalted Jesus will be the very center of worship. All will recognize and glorify Him for Who He really is.

John says the same, as the once slain but now living Lamb is worshiped by untold numbers of angels and others in heaven near the end of time (see Rev. 5:6-14):

> "Worthy is the Lamb, who was slain,
> to receive power and wealth and wisdom and strength
> and honor and glory and praise!" (Rev. 5:12).

So the resurrection of Jesus, leading to His exaltation, is connected indispensably to the subject of praise and worship. It is the heart of why Jesus is worshiped in

> The resurrection of Jesus is connected indispensably to the subject of praise and worship.

the first place, for, apart from the resurrection, there would be absolutely no reason to sing His praises. Every time we praise His name and every time we lift our voices to proclaim His glory, we give witness to the greatest single event in history. And with Paul, we proclaim:

"Death has been swallowed up in victory."
"Where, O death, is your victory?
Where, O death, is your sting?" (1 Cor. 15:54-55).

APPLICATION

We have seen that the same resurrection power that raised Jesus from the dead is available to believers through the internal work of the Holy Spirit. Further, Jesus' current position as High Priest and Mediator provides additional grounds for conquering sin and offering our lives to God. In short, God does not abandon us to live the Christian life but provides several means to assist us in reaching our goals. As a result, we can be controlled by the Holy Spirit, praising the exalted Son of God, rather than being ruled by our sinful passions. Several points of personal application follow.

First, there is a significant relationship between the availability of God's awesome resurrection power and the actual presence of Jesus Christ Himself in the believer's life through the work of the Holy Spirit. Jesus taught that the coming of the Holy Spirit provided a distinct advantage for the disciples (John 16:7). He thought the Holy Spirit would really be present in the believer's life. Paul pointed out that, in the Person of the Holy Spirit, Jesus Christ Himself is present in the believer (Eph. 3:16-17). Similarly, Christ lives in us through the Holy Spirit, producing the power to end the control of our sinful natures (Rom. 8:9-11).

It is plain that, for Jesus and Paul, this is a doctrine to be experienced. To take these teachings at face value is to realize that there is an actual, vital power that is imparted to the believer. To avail ourselves of such is to experience the very power of the risen Christ Himself.

The present working of God in the life of the believer is not simply wishful thinking; it is a fact. Christians are promised the same power that raised Jesus from the dead.[6] Just as the resurrection is a fact, so we have evidence of

> There is an actual, vital power that is imparted to the believer—the very power of the risen Christ.

the power available to us. So the first step is to fully recognize both the reality and the availability of the Holy Spirit's presence. It is as real as was the power that raised Jesus from the dead in actual, space-time history.

Second, in spite of this clear teaching of Scripture, Christians frequently seem to be caught between believing this doctrine and wondering where the power is in their own lives. Why doesn't this relationship appear more real in everyday contexts? I would like to address a few thoughts to this general concern.

One reason for the lack of recognition of this reality is that believers often do not cultivate this relationship. We spend too little quality time practicing Christian disciplines like prayer, thanksgiving, Bible study, fasting, true worship, simplicity, and biblical meditation.[7]

It is difficult to say why total commitment to the Lord seems to be lacking among believers. We will simply raise a question here. How strong a human relationship would exist between us and our husband, wife, children, or best friend if we devoted as much time and energy to them as we currently do to the Lord? So often, we expect the Lord to grant all of our needs, including experiencing His presence, but we are not willing to pay the price of developing and maintaining a steady relationship. The teaching of Scripture is that experiencing the reality of

> So often, we expect the Lord to grant all of our needs but are not willing to pay the price.

God's presence and power comes from walking with Him (1 John 2:6). This is a process that requires quality time.

Another crucially important consideration is to understand what Scripture means by God's presence in our lives. It is certainly possible that lacking a sense of God's power may be nothing more than the believer's own perspective — which may depend more on our own vantage point, mood, or current state of mind than on reality. Like the child who so easily forgets the last time their parents did something for them when the parent can name daily times of interaction, so we often concentrate on what we wish the Lord would do instead of remembering what He has already done. Even as adults, we tend to be unthankful and forgetful with regard to our heavenly Father.

Sometimes believers are upset because they can't *feel* God's power. But conversely, haven't we all felt much closer to the Lord on days when things were just naturally going well? But this is not a matter that is based on our emotions. Jesus *was* raised from the dead by God's power. Emotional matters need to be weeded out or they could constantly be a threat to the believer's spiritual well-being, depending on whether we are up or down. And woe to those who just have a more negative outlook on life! If we continue to tell ourselves that God's power is not real, there is no question that it will *seem* so. It will be our mind-set. This will overshadow any actual experience.

Just because we cannot physically observe the workings of the spiritual world, this does not indicate that it is not real. Sometimes we can learn from Christian fiction like C.S. Lewis's space trilogy[8] or Frank Peretti's recent volumes[9] that graphically depict not only how spiritual forces influence this world, but how human beings are basically unaware of the interplay in their own lives.

To sum up briefly: the reality of God's power is not the issue; He has proven as much by raising His Son from the dead. The power is there — we don't need to work ourselves up to a certain level. So whether or not we feel this reality is a moot point. Jesus and Paul promised it for the believer. A key is whether we will take the time and energy to cultivate the personal relationship that is already a reality in the believer's life.

Third, then how can Christians actually implement this power? For example, how can we overcome sin in our lives? As William Backus points out, the key is not for the Christian to attempt to exercise greater self-control or by struggling for more and more willpower. While it is true that Scripture constantly implores the believer to change sinful behavior, it is never left up to their own self-power.[10]

> The biblical emphasis is on conforming our mind and will to God's.

The biblical emphasis is on conforming our mind and will to God's. Paul gives this prescription: "Let God transform you into a new person by changing the way you think" (Rom. 12:1-2, NLB). As the apostle clearly says, the key here is altering our thinking patterns. Can we reach a point *where we no longer even desire improper behavior?* We already discussed a mind-transforming pattern of thinking from Philippians 4:6-9. Practicing such a method can alter our anxieties, attitudes, and outlooks, producing God's peace (vv. 7,9).

We can also use Paul's method to change our thinking about sin, correcting our many mistaken notions about it. Paul describes those who rebelled against God this way: "Instead of believing the truth about God, they deliberately chose to believe lies" (Rom. 1:25, NLB). We need to drive home the truth about sin being a struggle from within. Just as thinking thoughts from God's perspective strengthens us, availing ourselves of God's transforming power, so allowing ourselves to think sinful thoughts weakens us, often leading us into further sinning.

> We need to scrap the idea that sin can be indulged in and then quickly abandoned, with no ill effects.

We need to scrap the idea that sinful thinking can be indulged in and then quickly abandoned, with no ill effects. We must be constantly aware of this addictive power of sin so we do not even grant it small victories. Adjusting our thinking to the truth is a big part of the victory.

But is this just another way to say that believers must use their own power to turn from sin? Actually, Paul already addressed this question earlier in the same book. He states that it is the believer's obligation to work to achieve God's will, although he concludes that it is actually God who works in us (Phil. 2:12-13). Since the power is God's (3:10), Paul could not be saying that Christians are striving in their own power. Yet, the believer is still constantly encouraged to bring his will into accordance with God's desires and to act accordingly so that God might work through Him.[11] When we change our thinking and then our actions, God has promised to work through us.

We have also said that a positive motivation for avoiding sin is more powerful than a negative approach (although both can be useful), and far better than a legalistic one (which should not be used). For instance, I think a husband has far stronger reasons for avoiding lust when he acts out of his deep love for his wife and children, not wanting to cause them pain, rather than repeating to himself that such actions are wrong.

What motivation would provide the desire to avoid sin in general? What is more stimulating than obeying the lure of the flesh? Scripture suggests that one reason for implementing God's power to overcome sin in the Christian life is the longing for eternity.

> A husband has far stronger reasons for avoiding lust when he acts out of love, rather than simply because he knows such actions are wrong.

Immediately after Paul explains that he wants to know the power of Christ's resurrection, he says it is for the purpose of conforming himself to Christ so that he might attain the resurrection of his body (Phil. 3:11). As we have said, nothing should be as meaningful or as exciting as living the good life. God offers the opportunity to live the good life *forever* – a rather outstanding offer! Regularly throughout the New Testament, the believer is implored to act with a view towards heaven. In fact, all of life should be seen from this eternal outlook.

How does this translate into a motivation to avoid sin? Although some help may be provided from concentrating on the negative consequences of sin, I doubt that this is the best angle from which to fight. Rather, I think the strongest position for attacking the problem is to *prefer* something else even more. The ideal path would be to develop a greater desire for God and the peace He gives us now, as well as His future blessings in heaven. If I truly placed God and His Kingdom first in my life, I would be in the best position to conquer sin.

Why is this the case? Here is the key: **Sin's enticements are defeated if I prefer something else even more than sin, and act on it.** Victory comes from the believer's transformation. **To desire God and His eternal blessings, seeking them above all else, is to avoid sin for the sake of a greater love.** And we are motivated by those things we love most (Matt. 6:21,24).

We have called this the "top-down" perspective. We have applied it to the subjects in some of our other chapters. How about here? Does Scripture ever encourage believers to use an eternal motivation to conquer sin or to withstand temptation? Actually, several examples could be provided. Jesus taught that by placing our treasures in heaven rather than on earth, we could have the best perspective from which to deal with anxiety (Matt. 6:19-34). He also warned against the lure of materialism in His teaching that gaining possession of the entire world was not a fair trade for one's soul (Mark 8:36-37).

> To desire God and His eternal blessings, seeking them above all else, is to avoid sin for the sake of a greater love.

Paul placed earthly desires like glory-seeking and living for our appetites up against our present citizenship in heaven, saying that Christians seek the resurrection of their bodies (Phil. 3:18-21). Asserting that loving money leads to all sorts of evil (1 Tim. 6:10), Paul also provided instructions concerning the compassionate use of our wealth in light of eternity (6:17-19). In Hebrews we learn that ancient heroes were guided throughout their lives, avoiding all sorts of problems, by their eternal hope (Heb. 11:8-12,13-16,32-38). Moses, for example, successfully shunned sin by keeping his eye on his reward, knowing that it surpassed all of Egypt's treasures (11:24-27).

Therefore, in these passages believers were encouraged to overcome temptations such as anxiety, materialism, worldliness, the love of money, and other sins by developing a heavenly motivation. We have already seen how evangelism, doubt, persecution, suffering, and even death itself were to be seen from this "top-down" perspective. In short, the Christian should find God and His heavenly Kingdom to be sufficient motivation to overcome sin and live as we ought.

In conclusion, power is provided to the believer both to overcome sin and to live triumphantly. This is not just theoretical but was demonstrated in time-space history when the same power raised Jesus from the dead. Christians should cultivate a relationship with God through the Holy Spirit, relying not on feelings but on God's promise to work that power through the believer's life.

Victory over sin is actually a by-product of yielding our will to God so He can work through us. We begin by learning the truth about sin and progressively changing our thinking. Motivation is provided by both the new desire

> Victory over sin is a by-product of yielding our will to God.

to transform our thinking from nonbiblical thoughts to God's thoughts, which produces peace in this life (Phil. 4:6-9), and by the prospect of spending eternity with God in heaven. It is no coincidence that, when speaking of God's resurrection power available to Christians (Phil. 3:10), Paul places the entire discussion in the context of single-mindedly pressing onwards that he might attain his heavenly prize (3:7-13).

So from start to finish, these subjects are inextricably related. The power of the resurrection is available to believers so that they might grow in their relationship to God through the Holy Spirit, overcome sin, gain peace, and press on to their eternal home. Praise and worship to the God who has performed this in us should follow. In short, power is provided to train our thinking so that we do not even will to sin, since this would militate against our single-minded pursuit of the heavenly rewards offered by God (1 Cor. 9:24-27). Praise Him!

What could be more exciting and desirable than God's peace in the present, followed by spending eternity in fellowship with Jesus Christ, the Creator and Sustainer of the universe, and with our believing loved ones? If we believe and act on this, we are well on our way to conquering temptation and the practice of sin, since we now have a greater love from which to be motivated!

NOTES

1. Some examples can be found in Mark 14:62; Acts 2:22; 8:13; Rom. 1:16; 8:38; 1 Cor. 1:24; 2 Cor. 12:12; 1 Pet. 3:22.

2. I think that Paul's analogy in this and other similar passages below is concerned with water baptism. However, even if it is believed to be the baptism of the Holy Spirit, this does not necessarily change the main point being made here.

3. It should be briefly noted that the doctrine of the perseverance of the saints (or "eternal security") is not being discussed here. But interestingly, the writer of Hebrews defines true faith as that which continues to the end (Heb. 3:14; 10:39).

4. The Greek indicates that she was hanging on to Jesus (see the NASB, NIV, NKJV), not that Jesus wouldn't allow her to touch Him.

5. Some scholars think that this is the clearest example in the New Testament of Jesus being called God.

6. We looked at Rom. 6:4-14, 8:9-11; Gal. 2:20; Eph. 1:18-21; 3:16-17; Phil. 3:10; Col. 2:11-14.

7. The two most widely cited texts on this subject are Dallas Willard, *The Spirit of the Disciplines: Understanding How God Changes Lives* (San Francisco: Harper and Row, 1988); and Richard Foster, *Celebration of*

Discipline: The Path to Spiritual Growth (San Francisco: Harper and Row, 1988).

8. See especially C.S. Lewis's *Perelandra* (New York: Macmillan, 1944) and *That Hideous Strength* (New York: Macmillan, 1946).

9. See Frank E. Peretti, *This Present Darkness* (Westchester: Crossway Books, 1987) and *Piercing the Darkness* (Westchester: Crossway Books, 1989).

10. William Backus, *Finding the Freedom of Self-Control* (Minneapolis: Bethany, 1987), see especially the Introduction.

11. Ibid., pp. 48-52 and Chapter 8. Cf. William Backus and Marie Chapian, *Why Do I Do What I Don't Want To?* (Minneapolis: Bethany, 1984).

SUGGESTED READINGS

Backus, William. *Finding the Freedom of Self-Control.* Minneapolis: Bethany, 1987.

Backus, William, and Marie Chapian. *Why Do I Do What I Don't Want To?* Minneapolis: Bethany, 1984.

Hanson, G. Walter. "Resurrection and the Christian Life in Paul's Letters." In *Life in the Face of Death: The Resurrection Message of the New Testament.* Ed. by Richard N. Longenecker. Grand Rapids: Eerdmans, 1998.

Willard, Dallas. *The Spirit of the Disciplines: Understanding How God Changes Lives.* San Francisco: Harper and Row, 1988.

Reflecting on Lesson Five

1. If Justin had come to you for counsel, what advice would you have given him? Do you think you could have helped him to work his way out of the maze of sin, by the power of the Holy Spirit?

2. Evaluate the differences between the view that sin comes from outside us, and the New Testament teaching that it has more to do with what we

allow into our hearts. What are the implications here for understanding and conquering it?

3. In your own words, connect God's power in us, Jesus' work as our High Priest, and our worship. How are they related? How does the New Testament link them all to the resurrection of Jesus?

4. For group discussion: How do you think our own moods, emotions, and outlooks affect what we think God is doing in our lives? Do we numb ourselves to God's work? Do you agree with the analogy of unthankful children?

5. What affect do you think practicing the Christian disciplines and spending quality time with God might have on helping us to turn away from sin?

6. For group discussion: How do you evaluate positive versus negative motivation as encouragements to both live triumphantly and avoid sin? How could both be very helpful? Can it be said that one is stronger than the other? Why or why not?

7. Do you agree that the practice of sin can be defeated if we believe and practice a greater, more satisfying truth? If we truly prefer God and heaven above sin, do you think we have a powerful weapon with which to defeat sin?

Consider this:

Read 1 Corinthians 15:32. This is a profound statement: If there is no resurrection of the dead, we have no basis for behaving in a Christlike manner! How do standards for our behavior relate to the hope of the resurrection?

6

THE CHRISTIAN ETHICS OF TOTAL COMMITMENT

In this lesson:

▶ The concept of absolute commitment to Christ
▶ Good works as a response to the resurrection
▶ The measure of our love
▶ True love and true faith in action

In 1937, neoorthodox theologian Dietrich Bonhoeffer wrote his classic volume, *The Cost of Discipleship*. Grace is costly, he explains, as we suffer for truth. For some, it is "the grace of martyrdom." God's call is to total, unreserved allegiance to Jesus: "When Christ calls a man," wrote Bonhoeffer, "he bids him come and die."[1]

Bonhoeffer was arrested in 1943 for his involvement in the German underground, believing that opposition to Adolf Hitler was his Christian duty. He spent a couple of years in German prisons and concentration camps. Much of his time was used in ministering to other prisoners, who saw him as an incredible inspiration. But this book took on a new meaning after Bonhoeffer's death at the concentration camp at Flossenburg, Germany, in 1945, where he was hung.[2]

It has always amazed me that, in over sixty years, evangelicals have written nothing more forceful on the subject of the Christian call to total commitment. Whatever happened to preaching and teaching that are centered in wholehearted surrender to Jesus Christ? Why does it sometimes seem that believers are satisfied to bring people to Christ without challenging them to move on to total dedication to Him? Is it that we allow other things to crowd out our first love?

We said in the last chapter that daily power in the Christian life does not come from gritting our teeth and buckling down in our own strength. Rather, the key is allowing God's power to work through us by the constant transforming of our minds and approaching life from God's eternal, heavenly perspective.

From this biblical view, then, overcoming sin and living the victorious Christian life should be viewed as normal desires of the transformed life. In other words, my *chief* motivation for shunning sin should not be the negative angle that it is wrong (although this is often helpful). Rather, I should *prefer* to change my thinking from the positive perspectives of desiring God, achieving His peace, and securing His future bless-

> I should yearn to place God and His heavenly Kingdom first in my life.

ings in heaven. Thus I should yearn to place God and His heavenly Kingdom first in my life.

This, in turn, means that victory over sin is a product of God's transformation of the believer. The lure of sin is defeated if something else is preferred above it. To desire God and His blessings above all is to avoid sin simply because of having a greater motivation.

So our former subject was largely concerned with the daily power that God has made available to the believer to live for Him, including overcoming sin. Now we press on to the next area. Christians should progress onwards, still by God's power, to a life of full commitment to Him. Here, too, believers do not accomplish this in their own strength. The resurrection of Jesus is once again the focal point.

UNTO GOOD WORKS

We have already looked at Paul's teaching that, through Jesus Christ, the believer died to sin and rose with Him to a new life, no longer to serve the old nature.[3] In Romans 7:4, Paul refers to this idea, adding that the result of the transformation is that Christians should bear fruit. Since we now belong to God, who raised Christ from the dead, we should be committed to Him.

A related idea is voiced in 2 Corinthians 5:14-15. Following a lengthy discourse on the heavenly perspective from which we should view persecution, suffering, and death (4:7–5:10), Paul remarks that the love of Christ is evident in His death and resurrection. The result is that Christians died with Christ and should now live, not for themselves, but for Him.

Paul pursues similar themes elsewhere. In Romans 14:7-9, the apostle explains that we do not live or die unto ourselves, but

unto the Lord. Christ died and was raised, for the express purpose of being the Lord of both the living and the dead.
Therefore, since He is our Master, we are not to judge others, for
each of us must answer before the judgment seat of God (vv. 10-
12). In 1 Corinthians 6:13-14, he adds that we are not to mistreat
our bodies, since they should be given to a far higher calling —
the service of God. After all, God will raise our bodies like He
raised Jesus. In both of
these texts, the truth of
the resurrection is linked
with Christian behavior.
Ethics, too, is based on
this grand event.

> We are not to mistreat our
> bodies, since they should be
> given to the service of God.

God saved sinners, making them alive in Christ even while
they were still dead in sin. Then God raised up believers with
Christ in order to glorify and further bless them throughout eternity. So the entire process is a gift of God by means of His grace
and faith. Salvation is not due in any way to a person's good
works. Still, Paul carefully points out that believers were saved in
order to perform good works *afterwards* (Eph. 2:1-10).

Passages like these teach that just as Christians died to sin in
Jesus' death and were raised to a new life in His resurrection,
believers are now to commit their lives to God to bear the fruit
of good works. More than a victory over sin is involved here.
Even as great as that is, Christians are instructed to press on to a
new lifestyle.

In 1 Corinthians 15, Paul's subject for the entire discourse is
Jesus' resurrection and the resurrection body of believers. There
are few ways that Paul could have connected this subject to
Christian ethics more closely than he did in verses 30-32. After
discussing the believers' resurrection (which depends on Jesus'

being raised, vv. 17-23), Paul makes a simply startling statement. He claims that if the dead are not raised, believers have no ethical duties to suffer and die for their faith. In fact, they may as well eat and drink; no further demands are necessary before we die!

Paul's point appears to be that even living the Christian life depends on the truthfulness of Jesus' resurrection. Otherwise, we ought not feel compelled to give our lives for the sake of the gospel. Even more, believers can otherwise just "go party," since there is no ultimate Christian meaning in life. We might as well affirm another philosophy or religion.

> If the dead are not raised, believers have no ethical duties to suffer and die for their faith.

Just like theology, then, practicing the Christian life either stands or falls with Jesus' resurrection. This event is foundational, making a tremendous difference not only in what we believe, but also in what we do. One could hardly state more clearly or essentially the true meaning of this miracle.

As if to accent this twofold point, Paul ends his lengthy discourse by once again linking the resurrection to both theory and practice. He describes the connection between Jesus' resurrection and that of believers, concluding with a beautiful description of the believer's immortality (15:42-57). Then Paul explains that it is precisely because of this message that they should stand firmly and give themselves fully to the Lord's work, without wavering. Since our final resurrection is assured, we know that our work in the Lord is not ineffective (v. 58).

Interestingly, Paul concludes that work for the Lord is not vain. This is the same word (*kenos*) that he used three times earlier (vv. 10,14–twice), to say that Christian theology would be in vain if Jesus had not been raised from the dead. It is almost as if he were returning to that earlier theme to say that, not only is Christian theology not empty, but neither is our work for God. It all follows from the truth of Jesus' resurrection.

So our conclusion is not just that the believer should be committed to doing good works for the Lord. The reason we should be involved in service is that Jesus has been raised from the dead, and we will be, too. Because of our eternal hope in Christ Jesus, we are called to radical commitment to Him.

> The reason we should be involved in service is that Jesus has been raised from the dead, and we will be, too.

TOTALLY SURRENDERED

After Paul ended his discourse on the resurrection by encouraging believers to give themselves to the Lord's work (1 Cor. 15:58), he immediately turned in the very next verse to a practical example of one way that could be done. He asked the church at Corinth to take up a collection every Sunday, at least partially for the purpose of supporting poor Christians at Jerusalem (1 Cor. 16:1-4).

Scripture teaches that the Christian's life should be completely surrendered to God. Sometimes we express this today in terms of giving our time, talents, and treasures to the Lord. Paul apparently thought that there was a direct connection between Jesus' resurrection, the believer's resurrection, being committed to the Lord, and the matter of supplying the needs of others. In another passage (2 Cor. 8:1-7), he compliments the Macedonians for giving themselves first to the Lord, and then to others, in spite of their poverty.

When Jesus was asked to identify the greatest commandment, He answered that the first was to love the Lord *with our entire being*. The second greatest command was to love our neighbor *as much as we do our own selves* (Matt. 22:34-40). So this "top-down perspective" places God first and our responsibility to others second.

Answering a question regarding eternal life, Jesus affirmed a lawyer's response that the love of God and one's neighbor were of paramount importance (Luke 10:25-28).[4] When asked to identify who our neighbor was, Jesus responded by telling the parable of the Good Samaritan. The theme was that we should provide for those in need, even when it costs us time and money, and even when the needy ones are despised in society (vv. 29-37). Jesus then concluded with the convicting words that we should go and act similarly (v. 37).

These are some of the clearest passages that explain what it means to be totally surrendered to God. Believers are to commit themselves first to God and then to others as to themselves. Both of these charges are radical, too. But we might easily read past these points due to our familiarity with the texts. The first command involves loving God preeminently and with our entire being. Just in case we miss one of these words, Jesus included four qualifiers. We are to love God with all of our heart, all of our soul, all of our strength, and all of our mind (Luke 10:27a). Can there be any question that He was calling for our total allegiance to God?

Jesus' parable shows that the second greatest command was also taxing. We should love our neighbor as much as we do ourselves (10:27b). To make sure we get this point, Jesus chooses a story where the righteous man was required to help out at a very sizable expense to himself. He began by taking his life in his own hands since the robbers could well have remained nearby.

Then he gave his personal funds and interrupted his schedule —
all for a man that his society was highly prejudiced against. To
practice these two precepts would indeed be life changing!

But do we practice these two commands that Jesus called the
greatest? Earlier we asked what has happened to the biblical
teaching of total
commitment. Isn't   Do we practice the two commands
it the case that we   that Jesus called the greatest?
seldom value God
and His Kingdom
above all else (Matt 6:33)? Yet, Jesus warned us that we reveal
the true intentions of our heart by how we respond to this teaching (Matt. 6:21,24).

And what about our love for others — do we even come close
to treating them as we do ourselves? Throughout Scripture we
find the clear command to assist anyone in need, particularly the
poor and needy.[5] Paul instructs us to take the opportunity to do
good whenever we can, especially to fellow believers (Gal. 6:10).

One of the most convicting texts in all of Scripture is 1 John
3:17. Most believers are probably made periodically aware of situations where other Christians are truly in need. But John asks a
deeply challenging question here — how can we claim to have
experienced the love of God if we are able to do something but
just don't meet those needs? Few passages strike closer to the
heart.[6] Jesus (Matt. 25:34-46) and Paul (Gal. 6:10) teach that we
should treat everyone this way, not just believers. Do our lives
evidence this kind of fruit?

Christians are probably more aware of Jesus' first command
concerning loving God. This doesn't mean that we obey it,
though. And the second one regarding our neighbor should still
be placed above many lesser priorities that we so often elevate

above it. Love of others is not tangential; it occupies a place of importance behind only the command to love God with our entire being. A sobering thought here is that it must truly be love that motivates our actions. Any other reason is not only misplaced, but meaningless (1 Cor. 13:3).

APPLICATION

In the last two chapters we have examined connections between the resurrection of Jesus and daily power in the Christian life. We saw that the same power that raised Jesus from the dead is available to overcome sin and to live a life of good works in a manner that is fully committed to God, without ignoring love for our neighbor either. A few practical points might be made here.

First, it would seem that the connection is seldom made between Jesus' resurrection and the ethics of total commitment. But Paul's point in 1 Corinthians 15:32 is that it is precisely because of this event that believers practice some things and shun others. Since the risen Christ is Lord of our lives, His actions and teachings set the pattern for our behavior (Rom. 14:7-12; 1 Cor. 6:13-14). Further, the truth of the resurrection means that we ought to both stand firm in the faith and be committed to the work of the Lord (1 Cor. 15:58).

Many believers treat the evidence for Jesus' resurrection as an end in itself.

Yet, it seems that many believers treat the tremendous historical evidence for Jesus' resurrection as an end in itself. We sometimes do not notice either that such awesome power is still available for our life or that its truth leads naturally to total commitment to God. We should not stop with apologetic theory. We should pursue the resurrection all the way to practical applications in the ethics of radical surrender to God. The resurrection stands in all its display of God's power and majesty, beckoning to the Christian: "Since you know it is true, *do* something about it!"

Second, in speaking of Jesus' twofold command to love God and our neighbor, we should be reminded of the nature of love. While it is often said that words are cheap, we could also say that love "puts its money where its mouth is."

In the New Testament Jesus taught us that Christians should be known by their love for one another. It is our distinguishing mark (John 13:34-35). To express biblical love is to do more than to merely make a statement. Love involves obedience (John 14:15,21). Ultimate love is to die for another (John 15:13). We should even love our enemies (Matt. 5:44).

> Love "puts its money where its mouth is."

John goes as far as to say that if we don't love each other, we don't know God (1 John 4:7-8). This kind of love will express itself in sharing our possessions and meeting each others' needs. After all, love is more than a word; it involves action (1 John 3:17-18). It might even require us to die for another believer (1 John 3:16).

James comments similarly with regard to faith. Like John, if we are not willing to share our possessions, we are not expressing biblical faith (Jas. 2:14-17). Even the demons believe, but true faith manifests itself in our actions. Otherwise it is worthless (vv. 19-20).

Paul explains further that true love is humble, but not envious, proud, self-seeking, or angry. It doesn't rejoice inwardly when something bad happens to someone; it doesn't keep a list of past wrongs. Yet, if this kind of love is not present, all of our work for the Lord is in vain (1 Cor. 13:1-7)! How convicting! What a series of tough tests! The teaching in this passage is so loaded, it demands some very careful and prayerful unpacking.

So New Testament love is not easy to exercise; it is more than simply not hating someone. It certainly involves God's power and enablement. Yet, we are told to love both God and our neighbor with this self-sacrificial love. After all, we have the ultimate example — God loved us enough to send His only Son to die for us (John 3:16; 1 John 4:9-10).

> Faith manifests itself in our actions, or it is worthless.

Third, do we really take all of these New Testament commands seriously? Why are we so indifferent towards them? Why is it so difficult to get started? Do we place too much emphasis on coming to Christ and too little on growth? Or is it something else altogether?

In my opinion, one of the major problems among believers today is materialism. Most western Christians know the strain of overextending themselves by spending beyond their means. Not only do we often have very little for the Lord, but we also experience the "I gave at the office" attitude. Once we have paid some small amount to the Lord, we often struggle with giving more, even when we see real needs. But somehow, we always have enough for the night out with friends, new (name brand?) clothing, or our favorite hobby! What will it take for us to get our financial (and other) priorities straightened out so we can be faithful to our Lord's commands?[7]

Have we lost sight of our Lord's teachings? Are they really a priority as He instructed that they should be? I think that the two commandments that Jesus called the most important often slip to a lesser position. But then, as Jesus said, sometimes our words and actions betray the true intent of our heart (Matt. 6:21,24).

NOTES

1. The first English edition was published in 1948. Dietrich Bonhoeffer, *The Cost of Discipleship*, Revised Edition, tr. by R.H. Fuller (New York: Macmillan, 1959), p. 99.

2. I make no judgment concerning whether Bonhoeffer's political activism was a type of Christian ministry. Even some in the German church separated the two. Christians today would also disagree among themselves. Rather, I am referring strictly to the challenging exhortation to total surrender to Christ, to which the volume calls believers.

3. See Rom. 6:4-14; 8:9-11; Col. 2:11-14; cf. Gal. 2:20.

4. There is some difference of opinion as to whether this passage in Luke is parallel to Matt. 22:34-40 and Mark 12:28-34 (see previous paragraph). But this does not affect our comments.

5. For just a small sampling, see Lev. 23:22; Deut. 14:28-29; 15:7-11; Ps. 41:1-3; 72:12-13; Prov. 21:13; Matt. 6:2-4; 25:34-46; Luke 12:33; 1 Tim. 6:17-19; Jas. 2:15-17.

6. This is especially the case when the New Testament doesn't seem to allow the excuse that we just don't have enough to share. There are too many texts teaching that *whatever* was owned was shared with those in need (Matt. 10:42; Acts 2:45; 4:32-35; Jas. 2:15-17).

7. It is vitally important that we do some careful research before contributing to Christian organizations, not only because of the possible misuse of funds, but also to make sure that our giving fits our convictions as carefully as possible. Send for some literature, including an audited report from a reputable auditor. What is their chief goal? What percentage of the gift goes directly to the cause? What, exactly, are they trying to accomplish? Do they keep Jesus' two greatest commands in focus and balance? This last question is one of the most crucial. Our giving is one of the major areas that should reflect His teachings. Then, while praying for God's guidance but before making a final decision, call each ministry and ask some of the same questions. Try to gain a real sense of their mission. Does what they say agree with what they have written? To keep from covering the same preliminary information each time you call, befriend someone you can speak to whenever you have more questions or need more information. Lastly, follow up those organizations to whom you contribute. Are they continuing to do what they say? Do any others need to be added to your list? Keep important mailings and review them from time to time.

SUGGESTED READINGS

Bonhoeffer, Dietrich. *The Cost of Discipleship.* Revised Edition.
Tr. by R.H. Fuller. New York: Macmillan, 1959.

Getz, Gene. *A Biblical Theology of Material Possessions.*
Chicago: Moody, 1990.

Green, Joel B. "'Witness of His Resurrection': Resurrection,
Salvation, Discipleship, and Mission in the Acts of the
Apostles." In *Life in the Face of Death: The Resurrection
Message of the New Testament.* Ed. by Richard N.
Longenecker. Grand Rapids: Eerdmans, 1998.

MacDonald, William. *True Discipleship.* Kansas City: Walterick
Publishers, 1962.

Reflecting on Lesson Six

1. List some ethical issues where our decisions are informed by the truth of
    Jesus' resurrection. Show how relationships exist between this event and
    each of these matters.

2. Why do you think Jesus mentioned all four areas in Luke 10:27a? What
    do you think He was trying to emphasize by the overlap?

3. For group discussion: If the parable of the Good Samaritan was Jesus' pic-
    ture of the second command to love our neighbor, what picture might He
    have given if He had been asked to illustrate the first command to love
    God? Would His theme have been personal piety? Practicing the biblical
    disciplines? Telling others about the highest priority?

4. For group discussion: Have different people read 1 John 3:17-18, Mat-
    thew 25:34-46, James 2:14-17, and Galatians 6:10. How radical are

these commands to meet the needs of others? Why don't we fulfill them? What can we do to actually start?

5. Express in your own words the nature of New Testament love. What are its earmarks? What about the importance of the motives behind the actions?

6. Act out as a group: Make a list of people who have needs of various sorts. What can you do to meet those needs? Visit or call each one. Then divide up and do whatever can be done. When needed, arrange a long-term relationship to meet ongoing needs. If possible, combine physical labor with spiritual assistance. Who needs to know about God's greatest command?

7. For group discussion: Why do we seem to struggle so much in the area of finances? Why is it so difficult to obey New Testament commands? If God really was our first love, wouldn't we give far more than we presently do? What does this say about our real motivations?

Consider this:

Death is often a topic we avoid even thinking about, much less talking about, at all costs. Yet in preparation for Lesson Seven, consider death. What is the thing you most fear about death? Not knowing your future destination? Possible nonexistence? The pain and illness leading up to death? Leaving your loved ones behind? Think about how the hope of resurrection impacts your attitude toward death.

Resurrection: Heart of the Christian Life

7

FEAR OF DEATH

In this lesson:

▶ The causes of the fear of death
▶ How the hope of resurrection reduces that fear

Karen was a middle-aged, highly emotional woman, who was known to her friends as a strong Christian. During her last ten years or so, she had lived with the constant fear of getting cancer. Her father and two brothers had already had the disease and two of them had passed away. Every ache and pain turned into a "What if . . ." scenario for her, followed by a call to one of her friends, who would try to encourage her. Trips to the hospital for testing grew more and more common.

Then came the day she would never forget. Having a routine test for something entirely different, she was diagnosed with cancer. After further testing and days of apprehension, her doctor called her into his office for a consultation. His countenance gave him away before the conversation even started. "I really wish I had better news for you," he began. "Your cancer is a variety that is considered to be terminal."

Her friends and family braced themselves for the inevitable emotional outburst that they were sure would come. After all, hadn't Karen been a "basket case" over the years in regard to this topic? On several occasions, they remarked how they didn't think she would be able to handle the news if she was ever diagnosed with the dreaded disease. But now her worst fears had been realized.

But that time never came. Even after her worst fears had been realized, she took the news very well. Even more surprising, in the months to come, she only grew stronger. What very few of her friends knew was that she had done much recent study and contemplation on the subject of her fear. Her faith kicked in and, whether or not the cancer turned out to be terminal, she gave every appearance of being ready, secure in her beliefs. Neither was it just a passing trend. "I wish I had learned these things a lot earlier," she said one day. "I would have saved myself a lot of pain, regardless of the outcome."

> God frequently gives believers what might be called "dying grace," including a strange calming peace.

What had happened to Karen? Perhaps the greatest single lesson I have learned during my wife's death in 1995 and with several other loved ones since then is that God frequently gives believers what might be called "dying grace," including a strange calming peace. But curiously enough, it seldom appears before it is really needed.

There is no greater source of anxiety than the prospect of death. Why do we fear it? What does Jesus' resurrection have to say to these anxieties? We will also make some suggestions for reducing these fears in our everyday lives.

WHY DO WE FEAR DEATH?

Death is probably our ultimate fear. Its icy fingers affect not simply our thoughts about the topic itself, but so many other subjects that we deal with during life, such as sickness, loneliness, and questions of meaning. It is commonly portrayed that way in Scripture, as well, where it is a major theme in books like Job, Psalms, and Proverbs.[1]

Many passages in Scripture reveal an awareness of the agonizing anxieties concerning death. Not even saints are immune to these fears. In fact, Hebrews 2:14-15 records an incredibly direct claim. Jesus became a man and died so that, by His death, He could destroy the Devil's hold on death. By so doing, He provided the means to release those who were in slavery to the fear of death for their entire lives! Imagine that! Seen from one angle, Jesus' Incarnation was for the purpose of releasing us from the lifelong bondage of fearing death. Yes, not only is God aware of our foremost anxiety, but He took steps to combat that fear. He does care about us and our needs.

One example of a somewhat negative response to death is found in 2 Kings 20:1-11. There we find that King Hezekiah was very sick. Isaiah told him plainly that he should prepare for his own death (v. 1).

Hezekiah responded by praying to God and weeping bitterly (vv. 2-3). Even with his positive relationship to God, he did not welcome death. God heard Hezekiah's prayer. Hezekiah would be healed and 15 years would be added to his life (vv. 4-6). God even provided a sign of His promise in answer to the king's request — the time of day would be moved backwards (vv. 7-11). The episode with Hezekiah is not so surprising. Don't many of us respond to death in similar ways? So why do even believers fear death? Why does it seem to be the deepest of our anxieties? There are a number of possible responses to these questions.[2]

For some, death itself is not as bad as the conditions that sometimes accompany it. The pain often associated with dying is most fearful to some. Perhaps like Karen, watching loved ones suffer through cancer seems unbearable. Others are plagued by thoughts of bodily decomposition and funerals. Did you ever ride past a cemetery and feel uncomfortable?

The uncertainties of judgment after death even worry some believers. How can I be absolutely sure that when I appear before Jesus, He will acknowledge me as one of His children? There is sometimes a major irony here. It is often those who are most in love with the Lord who suffer the most at this point.

The plain, unavoidable fact of death itself probably scares the most people. Perhaps foremost on the list is that death involves a direct confrontation with the unknown. The fear of nonexistence is frightening, even repulsive. Doubts about the afterlife can be terrifying. Close on the heels of these huge anxieties is the pain of ending earthly relationships with loved ones and friends. And all of this must be faced alone — death is the one event where no one else can accompany us. From a human standpoint, it seems that we are utterly and finally isolated.

> The fear of nonexistence is frightening, even repulsive.

No one is exempt. You've probably often heard the popular saying: "The only assurances in life are death and taxes." Occasionally, some avoid some taxes. Unfortunately, none can bypass death. Unless the Lord comes in our lifetimes, we will each have our moment. Even believers struggle in this area. We need to be honest here: death is surely an enemy that cannot be whisked away by fancy talking or magic thinking. It is the most fearsome element of sin's curse.

But we need to be true to Scripture on the other end, too. Since Jesus came to relieve anxiety concerning death, as the New Testament tells us, then such a victory is at least possible. Does the Bible provide any hints for success?

JESUS' RESURRECTION AND THE FEAR OF DEATH

The passage in Hebrews 2:14-15 explains that by sacrificing His own life, Jesus destroyed the Devil's power over death. In this manner, those in bondage to the fear of death might be freed. While Jesus' resurrection is not mentioned specifically in this context, it is obviously implied. Otherwise, the conclusion would not follow. If Jesus had not been raised, then He provided no real remedy to the problem of death because He, too, would have finally succumbed to the reality of the grave. Only if He conquered death could it be said in any meaningful sense that He provided a real solution. Other references in the same book indicate that the writer of Hebrews is well aware of this and agrees wholeheartedly (7:23-25; 13:20-21).

> If Jesus was not raised, then He provided no real remedy to the problem of death.

Other New Testament passages make it quite

clear that the resurrection of Jesus is absolutely indispensable if we are to provide an answer to our dilemma. It is the ultimate response to death. While mentioning various reasons why people are afraid of dying, Scripture also responds directly to these fears. And Jesus' victory over death is at the very heart of the solution, too.

It is undeniable that pain is a frequent companion of death. Yet, we have seen in Chapter 4 that Paul counsels believers to focus their attention, not on the suffering, but on eternal life instead (2 Cor. 4:7-18). The reason for such an attitude is that our troubles are only momentary; they will be over soon. On the other hand, the afterlife is eternal and should be the object of our concentration (vv. 17-18). It should be noted that Paul's advice here is anchored firmly in the reality of Jesus' resurrection. The same God who raised Jesus from the dead will also raise believers (vv. 14).

Now at first thought, one might be tempted to think that such a teaching is of little practical value because it fails to ease the pain, which is quite real. Yet, I think that such a response fails for at least two reasons.

First, eternal life is a fact. Eternity is far better and lasts far longer than this life. This justifies the priority in both our thinking and our actions.[3] Paul's teaching here agrees with Jesus' heavenly perspective on placing God and His Kingdom first (Matt. 6:19-34). Although we sometimes suffer, Paul is correct *even if* the pain is not thereby lessened, because eternal life is still a reality long after the pain actually does subside. Although pain is real, we rarely recall its intensity when it is over.

> Eternity is far better and lasts far longer than this life.

Second, we have argued earlier that this heavenly perspective
can actually reduce the amount of our pain. We have all experienced how all it takes is an optimistic word from a doctor concerning the absence of a serious medical problem to immediately diminish our physical suffering. The reason for this is that
the emotional factor has been reduced. Similarly, a proper perspective on eternal life can take our mind off our immediate situation and give us the assurance that, at least in the long run,
everything will turn out all right (even eternally so!). That convic-
tion should cause us to relax and refocus our attention away
from the pain, lessening at least the emotional element.[4]

While thoughts of bodily decomposition, along with visions of
funerals and cemeteries, can also encourage us to think fearful
thoughts, we will maintain in the next section that the majority
of this sort of thinking is due directly to our incorrect thinking
patterns. As such, we can and should weed out thoughts like
these. When we exchange biblical thoughts for these painful
ones, we can gain victory over our distorted thinking.

Further, such fear is also factually misplaced because, as we
have said, eternal life is a fact. However nasty such scenarios may
seem, they cannot keep us from immediate consciousness after
death. We survive our own funerals and bodily decomposition!
And for believers, this is a blissful occurrence as well (2 Cor. 5:8).

Paul extends this last point even further in 1 Corinthians 15:53-
57. He asserts that after the believer's body is raised, death will
finally be conquered. The grave will possess no further control
over our destinies. It will have lost its bite (vv. 53-56). After saying this, Paul reminds us that this victory is ours because of what
Jesus Christ accomplished for us (v. 57). Once again, as in
1 Corinthians 4:14, it is Jesus' resurrection that paves the way for

the Christian's victory (vv. 45-49). As we have said before, Jesus' resurrection is God's trump card on suffering!

Standing before the judgment seat of Christ may cause some believers concern (2 Cor. 5:10). But Paul has just finished the point that, after death, the believer will be present with the Lord (v. 8; cf. Phil. 1:21-23), not rejected by Him. Christians will never be condemned (John 3:16-18,36; 5:24-29), due to Christ's actions on our behalf in His death and resurrection (Eph. 2:4-7).

Some readers may think that easy citations of biblical references like these denigrate the seriousness of the anxiety, but actually the exact opposite is true. It is precisely because we do not do a sufficient job of incorporating biblical truths like these into our lives that the anxiety itself can dominate us. We should remember that the *same* verses that tell us about judgment also tell us that Christians need not be concerned for their eternal life. Again, we will address practical concerns like these in our next section.

> Due to Christ's actions on our behalf, Christians will never be condemned.

So only the non-Christian need fear condemnation. Believers are never doomed. The answer for unbelievers is to trust the Lord in light of the gospel facts (2 Cor. 6:2) so the blessings of eternal life may apply to them, too. While there may still be some apprehension for the believer who fears meeting the Lord, it should be clear that our eternal destiny is never at stake. Actually, some timidity might actually work in our favor by keeping us from becoming proud or calloused (1 Cor. 10:12).

But doesn't death represent the greatest unknown we will ever experience? Yes, but Jesus also experienced it and rose from the dead. He didn't tell us a lot of details, but what He did say is extremely helpful. We can learn some important truths about heaven from the truth of His resurrection alone. We made a list of these in volume I.

The point here is that while Scripture certainly doesn't tell us everything about eternal life, we *do* know enough not to be so fearful about it. It is no longer the unknown realm. Since Jesus was *actually* raised from the dead, we already know the most important aspects that we need in order to calm our fears.

I think it is very encouraging to take what I have called a "Christmas morning" view of heaven. We have some good ideas what it will be like, but we will also be pleasantly surprised by its nature. This is a rewarding angle from which to view eternity, since it makes even those unknown elements something to be thankful for instead of something to fear. Since we know that even the mysteries will be positive, we can look forward to them. We can calm our fears with the truth.

> Since we know that even the mysteries will be positive, we can look forward to them.

Therefore, we do not have to worry about the threat of nonexistence. We know about Jesus' resurrection and enough details of heaven. Scripture confirms our immediate existence after death (Phil. 1:21-23; 2 Cor. 5:1-8). Besides, it is **absolutely impossible** that we could ever experience nonexistence, since there would be no "me" to experience the nothingness!

There are no magic words or evidences to change the fact that terminating relationships with our loved ones is exceptionally painful. Jesus wept beside Lazarus's tomb, even though He knew His friend would very shortly be raised from the dead. Watching the sisters was painful (John 11:33-36).

But Jesus' resurrection still brings ultimate victory, even here. While earthly relationships are temporarily discontinued by death, we are told that true knowledge of others will only come in the future life (1 Cor. 13:12). Believers will know each other and enjoy fellowship in heaven (Matt 8:11). And we will be with Jesus (2 Cor. 5:8; Phil. 1:23), seeing Him face to face (Rev. 22:4). Later we will be reunited with our believing family members and friends, either by death or by the coming of the Lord (1 Thess. 4:13-18). Jesus' resurrection is the key here, too (v. 14).

In sum, we do not attempt to make death into a friend.[5] It is a bitter pill to be swallowed; it hurts. Pain is not fun, even if we have an eternal perspective. And even temporary separation from loved ones, especially in cases where a parent still has children at home, is certainly emotionally painful. Undoubtedly, death is the greatest of all ills that we must face.

However, the most important factor is that, thankfully, there is more to death than this earthly reality. Death is the doorway to victory; it is the entrance to paradise. The bitterest of pills brings eternal health. The key in this entire discussion is that *ultimate* victory lies *only* on the other side of death. Paradoxically, while death is no fun, without it we cannot experience the best in life.

> Death is the doorway to victory; it is the entrance to paradise. The bitterest of pills brings eternal health.

This subject is certainly loaded with irony, but these things are nevertheless true. Death is the only door that leads to the fullest possible joy (Ps. 16:11). Death can *still* be gain and believers can *still* prefer to die and be with Christ (Phil. 1:21-23; 2 Cor. 5:8). But how do we get to that point?

APPLICATION

Few topics have more practical importance. Death and dying are simply subjects that concern everyone, whether we wish to think about them or not. By way of application, Jesus' resurrection provides an overall response, as well as some brief suggestions concerning how believers might implement biblical truths in their daily lives. While we cannot stop all intrusive thoughts about death, our goal will be to gain victory over the type of fear that leads to bondage.

First, the theme of our two volumes is that Jesus' resurrection is not just an occurrence with theoretical or hypothetical implications. In important matters like Christian doubt, grief, suffering, the need for daily power, and total commitment, as well as conquering the fear of death, this event provides the needed groundwork from which an effective strategy may be launched where we need it the most — in the real world.

More than once we have seen that Jesus provided counsel for those who grieved after the death of a loved one. When Lazarus died, Jesus comforted Martha with the practical meaning of resurrection — those who die in Christ still live (John 11:20-27). When He first spoke to his despairing disciples after His own death, He presented His resurrection body for their inspection (Luke 24:36-43; John 20:19-20). His appearance changed them from doubt and fear to joy and faith (John 20:20).[6]

Second, our main topic for application concerns how we can begin to gain victory over the type of fear that leads to bondage. We have already seen that Jesus came to provide a remedy for this sort of death anxiety (Heb. 2:14-15).

This does not mean that we can get to a point where the thought of our own death or that of a loved one does not bother us. Even Jesus was affected by the pain of separation and grief after the death of Lazarus; the Son of God wept (John 11:33-36). Paul says that Christians grieve, too, but not for the same reasons — we have an eternal hope through Jesus' resurrection (1 Thess. 4:14b-15). This distinction makes all the difference in the world. Our sorrow has limits. But Scripture tells us that we *can* be freed from the more dominating sort of anxiety. That kind of fear can be remedied.

I will begin by listing three steps that outline the approach I will take here: The believer must (1) be convinced that eternal life is a reality, (2) shift our thinking to God's heavenly, "top-down" perspective, and (3) replace our anxious thoughts with these biblical truths whenever

> Christians grieve, too, but not for the same reasons.

they arise. The *practice* of this truth can bring great relief from the debilitating aspects of the fear of death. We will address each of these points in turn.

The first key has already been provided in volume I. Jesus' resurrection from the dead gives us a strong, twofold argument for the believer's eternal life. This event signifies victory over death by its very nature. The resurrection appearances were foretastes of heaven. For forty days, heaven broke into earth, complete with the glory of God's new creation. So when His disciples saw Jesus after His crucifixion, they witnessed walking, talking, eternal life. Heaven stood in front of them, before their eyes.

Further, we pointed out that Jesus' central message was the Kingdom of God and the entrance requirements for eternal life. Therefore, if God validated any of Jesus' teachings by raising Him from the dead, this applies to His claims about the afterlife, since they were His chief focus.[7]

Since Jesus' counsel to those going through grief also focused on the truth of the resurrection, as do other New Testament texts that deal with this subject,[8] it is appropriate that we also start here in our attempt to face head-on the fear of death. For those interested, there are other strong arguments for the reality of life after death, too.[9]

So we must begin with the truth of eternal life, as Jesus did. And the resurrection is especially equipped to provide that foundation. Since I will live one second after death and even survive the dissolution of my physical body, I have no *ultimate* reason to fear its power. At the least, while viewing death as an enemy, I must not be overcome by anxiety regarding its reality.

But the truthfulness of eternal life must become more than just a sterile piece of knowledge in order for it to work on our emotions. So we will now return briefly to a subject that we have pursued throughout these two volumes. A second step in combating the fear of death is to view the entire subject from God's eternal perspective. Several dozen times, the New Testament encourages believers to seek God and His Kingdom above all else (Matt. 6:33). In general, the command is for us to set our hearts single-mindedly on heavenly truths rather than on the earthly concerns that dominate our lives (Col. 3:2). The top floor remains the same — God and His eternal Kingdom — and is applied to all our myriads of earthly needs, desires, and situations. Among other applications, this is said in a variety of ways that has a direct bearing on our fear of death.

> A step in combating the fear of death is to view the entire subject from God's eternal perspective.

The pursuit of heavenly treasures should replace the anxiety that we suffer regarding earthly interests (Matt. 6:19-34). Even gaining all the world has to offer us should not be exchanged for even one soul (Mark 8:36-37). Rather, we should use our wealth for the good of others, thereby laying up heavenly treasures (1 Tim. 6:17-19; cf. 6:10). Citizenship in heaven is our goal, not physical gratification (Phil. 3:18-21).

Even suffering and death should be viewed similarly. Death is the greatest of the anxieties that we face. As real as it is, we should get our mind off it by turning our thoughts toward eternal life (2 Cor. 4:14-5:10; Phil. 1:21-23). Persecuted believers were told to rejoice because Jesus' resurrection ensured their eternal life in heaven where their inheritance cannot perish or spoil (1 Pet. 1:3-9). The theme of Hebrews 11 is that the heroes of the faith spent their entire lives in pursuit of their eternal hope, which was far more meaningful than earthly goals (Heb. 11:8-10,13-16,24-27).

This heavenly (or "top-down") perspective is much more than a biblical teaching with which believers simply agree. It is a life-changing principle — perhaps the overarching guide for Christian ethics in all of Scripture. It is transforming because it frees us to pay far less attention to earthly concerns and worries like the budget, unpaid bills, human relationships, and even our health. Jesus' whole point in Matthew 6:19-34 is that if we are anxious concerning these daily issues, we actually betray ourselves by showing that these are our real treasures (vv. 19-21).

Of course we are finite creatures living in a hurting world. We cannot remove ourselves from the earth. But the central question here is the nature of our first love. The Christian life, then, is a balance between seeking first God and His Kingdom and then loving our neighbors as ourselves. Living the top-down, heavenly perspective is truly liberating because it not only frees us *from* life's many concerns, but it frees us to live *for* God. This is life indeed.

Living from a heavenly perspective frees us *from* life's many concerns and frees us to live *for* God.

Once we know eternal life is a reality, we need to *think* and *live* in terms of that reality. We must **pattern our lives according to top-down precepts.** Our lives as a whole need to reflect this heavenly way of thinking. In short, if living the highest quality of life for all eternity is really important to us, then it will motivate us. And if, with Paul, we are truly motivated to pursue this goal, it will direct our efforts, decisions, and actions. Even at the end of his life, Paul said he had not yet reached his heavenly target, so he constantly held it out before him, giving up everything else in order to attain it (Phil. 3:10-15).

Then what do we do with all of our fears about death? Now we have reached the third step. Once we are convinced of eternal life, and have re-oriented our thinking according to God's top-down outlook on life, we must apply these truths *deeply* within ourselves, in order to *practice* them in our thinking about death. As with Paul's general treatment of anxiety that we outlined in Chapter 3, we must face our worries by changing our thoughts to God's perspective (Phil. 4:6-9).[10]

Every single time we experience anxiety about death we need to pause briefly and replace the thought with a biblical one, perhaps regarding the reality of Jesus' resurrection, the glories of eternal life, or concerning the priority of laying up treasures in heaven. This weeding out process of our unbiblical thoughts is not easy, but its *practice* can correct and change our bad habits (Phil. 4:9).

How might it actually work in everyday life? Whenever we are suddenly confronted by an intruding thought about death, perhaps occasioned by hearing that someone has been diagnosed with a terminal illness, or driving past a cemetery, we need to immediately examine our thinking for the incorrect thoughts we have just told ourselves. Here are some examples: "That would be more difficult than I could ever bear." "What if, after all, there's no afterlife?" "I can't stand to think about death — I'll just ignore it."

In place of these lies, we need to forcefully substitute God's truth: "Just like Karen, this is not more than I could bear, with God's help. He will give me dying grace, but probably not a day before I really need it." "I *can* stand to think about death. In fact, the more I do so, the less it will hurt. But if I try to avoid thinking about it, it will become even more painful." "No, death is not my friend and it is not painless. But Jesus' resurrection proves that it does lead to eternal life in heaven, and that will be fantastic."

In sum, we need to (1) be convinced of the reality of eternal life, (2) reorient our thinking to that heavenly perspective in all of life, and (3) forcefully confront our anxious

> We must be convinced of the reality of eternal life, reorient our thinking to that heavenly perspective, and forcefully confront our anxious thoughts.

thoughts about death with God's truth. This needs to be *practiced* until it is an habitual way of thinking, as we weed out the incorrect thoughts and replace them on a *regular basis*. The more we rehearse the pattern, the better we'll get at it.

Once again, this is not some strategy that is foreign, either to Scripture or to sound thinking. God tells us that Jesus came to conquer the fear of death and to release us from this bondage. And God has given us some details about the reality of eternal life. He has repeatedly instructed us to set our thoughts on heaven, rather than on earthly things. And He has told us to deal with anxiety by the continual practice of changing our thinking, by trading lies for the truth. It *really does* work.

While apprehension about death may always be a concern, we can short-circuit the bondage-producing way of thinking. We can keep the fear of death from dominating our thoughts and lives. We can practice these truths. As Jesus did with Martha, Mary, and His grieving disciples, the starting point is the factual reality of the eternal life that He has provided. Those who believe in Him will live even at death (John 11:25) because they have *already* made the transition from death to life (John 5:24).

There is a widespread view that we can't really change "the way we are." But this is false and sadly so, because it can keep us from the victory that Jesus came to give us. He can free us from the debilitating aspects of death anxiety (Heb. 2:14-15). The more we practice, and the more forcefully we do so, the more control we will have over our thinking. And the less affect the fear of death will exert over us. Like medicine, it is simply wonderful to see Paul's method "kick in," leading to a new attitude and more of God's peace (Phil. 4:7,9). The key is to *practice forcefully* these truths at every opportunity — especially when the fear arises, but even when we don't need it — as a preventative measure. It is simply liberating!

As strange as it may sound, death is our doorway to victory, leading to paradise. The bitterest pill in our entire life brings eternal health. But *ultimate* victory lies *only* on the other side of death. Paradoxically, death is painful in more than one way, but only through it can we experience the best in (eternal) life!

NOTES

1. For Just a sampling, see Job 3:20-22; 5:26; 7:13-15; Ps. 6:5; 55:4-8; 88:1-18; 89:46-48; 116:15; Prov. 11:19; 14:32.

2. For a more detailed treatment, see Gary R. Habermas and J.P. Moreland, *Beyond Death: Exploring the Evidence for Immortality* (Wheaton: Crossway Books, 1998), Chapter 13; Gary R. Habermas, *The Resurrection of Jesus: An Apologetic* (Grand Rapids: Baker, 1980; Lanham: University Press of America, 1984), Appendix 3.

3. See Habermas and Moreland, *Beyond Death,* Section I for the evidence and Section III for some of the reasons for the priority of the afterlife in this life.

4. Even apart from eternal life, several recent studies have shown that pain is often quite manageable. See Albert Ellis and Michael Abrams, *How to Cope with a Fatal Illness: The Rational Management of Death and Dying* (New York: Barricade Books, 1994); Wayne D. Gersh, William L. Golden, and David M. Robbins, *Mind over Malignancy: Living with Cancer* (Oakland: New Harbinger Publications, 1997). Some spiritual discernment may be necessary in reading these volumes.

5. For an intriguing book that treats death as enemy, stranger, friend, mother, and lover, see Peter Kreeft, *Love Is Stronger Than Death* (New York: Harper and Row, 1979; San Francisco: Ignatius Press, 1992).

6. Details of Jesus' discussion with Martha are found in Chapter 4 above, while His approach to His disciples is located in Chapter 3.

7. For this argument, see *The Resurrection: Heart of New Testament Doctrine,* Chapter 4.

8. Even with the raising of Lazarus, the focus is on Jesus as the resurrection, not on the miracle itself (John 11:25-26). For other passages that also emphasize the truth of Jesus' resurrection in the context of death and grief, see John 20:19-20; 1 Cor. 15:45-57; 2 Cor. 4:7-18; 1 Thess. 4:13-18.

9. For a discussion of many such arguments, see Habermas and Moreland, *Beyond Death,* Section I.

10. Reviewing our discussion of Paul's four steps from Phil. 4:6-9 (Chapter 3) might be worthwhile before continuing the discussion here.

SUGGESTED READINGS

Habermas, Gary R., and J.P. Moreland. *Beyond Death: Exploring the Evidence for Immortality.* Wheaton: Crossway Books, 1998. Chapter 13.

Habermas, Gary R. *The Resurrection of Jesus: An Apologetic.* Grand Rapids: Baker, 1980; Lanham, MA: University Press of America, 1984. Appendix 3.

Kreeft, Peter J. *Love Is Stronger Than Death.* New York: Harper and Row, 1979; San Francisco: Ignatius Press, 1992.

_____. *Heaven: The Heart's Deepest Longing.* San Francisco: Harper and Row, 1980).

Nouwen, Henri J.M. *Our Greatest Gift: A Meditation on Dying and Caring.* San Francisco: Harper San Francisco, 1994.

Reflecting on Lesson Seven

1. What would you have been prepared to tell Karen if she had asked for your advice prior to her doctor's discovery of cancer? How would your advice have changed after the diagnosis?

2. For group discussion: What other reasons can you name for why we fear death? Which are the worst ones? Which are easier for you to handle? Why?

3. What significance do you see in Hebrews 2:14-15? Explain why this is a powerful promise for Christians.

4. What do you think Paul meant in Philippians 1:21-23? How is it a gain to die? How can it actually be better by far to die, even if we do go to be with Christ? Do you really believe this?

5. For group discussion: Do you really think that having an eternal perspective on life can actually lessen one's pain right now? Explain your answer.

6. For group discussion: In what ways is death an enemy? Are there any senses in which death is a friend?

7. For group discussion: How do you evaluate the strategy here for dealing with the worst aspects of death anxiety? What do you think are the strongest points? What are the weakest points, in your view?

8. Activity: Keep a journal of your thoughts about death. What unbiblical things do you tell yourself about it? With what biblical ideas can you counter each of these? (Or make a chart and list the improper thoughts on the left. Across from each one, list the corresponding counter truth.)

Consider this:

Can you think of other areas of life than the ones mentioned in this book where Christians need help in learning to walk in Christ's way? How can the resurrection of Jesus and the top-down perspective be applied to these areas to bring the power of God to bear in achieving success?

Summary Conclusion:
The Center of New Testament Practice

Jesus' resurrection energizes Christian practice. The New Testament applies this event widely, from overhauling our lives to soothing our daily hurts. It is astounding that this awesome event two millennia ago still offers the power to transform our quality of life! Then it guarantees heaven, too! What more could anyone ask from their faith?

Jesus' resurrection is the reason we practice the spiritual disciplines. We need to integrate this event with biblical meditation, prayer, fasting, worship, and simplicity, among others. Linking theory to practice can revolutionize our lives. Internalizing God's principles brings victory and peace, *even in the very toughest areas of life.*

In fact, I view much of this book as the relationship between Jesus' resurrection and exercising the Christian disciplines. Each chapter is specifically designed to introduce practices to bring us into a closer relationship with God, experiencing His peace.

APPLICATION: LESSONS TO LEARN

Two themes emerged most frequently. Both share a central idea — biblical prescription can alter our thinking, conforming us to God's truth. Paul charges: "Let God transform you into a new person by changing the way you think" (Rom. 12:1-2, NLT).

The first transformation pattern comes from Philippians 4:6-9. We saw Paul's four steps to countering anxiety: (1) prayer (v. 6); (2) thanksgiving (v. 6) and praise (v. 8b); (3) exchanging our anxious (or other unbiblical) thoughts for God's truth (v. 8); and (4) practicing truth until it is habitual. Every time an offensive thought intrudes, the process should be triggered. Obeying God's laws brings peace (Phil. 4:7,9). What a promise!

This process works because: "It is not, however, events either past or present which make us feel the way we feel, but our *interpretation of those events.*"[1] So the key to our feelings is *how we respond* to our surroundings. Our worst hurts come from what we tell ourselves, so our pain can be controlled! Changing our improper thoughts changes our painful emotions. Even when we can't affect our circumstances, we *can* change what *is* under our control. Amazingly, it is precisely this that causes our worst pain![2]

While desires like popularity or a new home are nice, they don't produce true happiness. God's truth needs to be *forcefully* applied to unbiblical thinking: our peace does *not* depend on what we *do* but on what God has done for us. His truth produces peace in this life. What more *must* we have on earth?

I have seen this process transform many lives. The recipe is to *tenaciously practice* replacing our unbiblical thoughts with God's truth until it becomes habitual. It probably won't stick the first time. When we retreat to our former thinking, we mustn't quit. Restarting the process, each success brings us one step closer to conquering emotional pain. Repetition produces resolve and momentum. Don't ever believe the lies that it won't work, or that it's too difficult. It is liberating! But nothing will happen until we apply God's standards.

The second transformation pattern is what we called the "top-down" perspective on life. The New Testament commands us to employ it in our daily struggles. It demands a little more advanced technique, building on the earlier approach as a prerequisite. Thus, we should rid our minds of unruly thoughts before moving to a higher mode.

The chief idea behind the top-down principle is that the "top floor" is unchanging — seek God and His Kingdom above all else

(Matt. 6:33). This truth should be applied to the "bottom floor," which changes frequently due to life's many concerns.

We should apply heavenly truth to earthly situations by consciously pursuing God's perspective, activating it everywhere. How is a particular issue affected by eternity? This outlook develops a lifestyle that Scripture encourages dozens of times. The resurrection is the reason we seek heavenly rather than earthly pursuits (Col. 3:1-4).

This heavenly perspective dictates that, *regardless* of what occurs, everything will *ultimately* turn out just fine. Instead of getting bogged down, we can choose to live *above* the daily grind. When this is practiced until it becomes part of us, we can streamline and simplify our lives. We move from getting stopped in our tracks by circumstances to learning how to apply heaven to earth. What does eternity say about life's issues?

We bring tremendous pain into our lives by unbiblical thinking. We may not realize how much until we have removed some of it. Leaving emotional suffering behind is absolutely life-changing. It eliminates pain and simplifies our lives by teaching us to concentrate on what is really valuable for eternity. It keeps us from being fragmented and allows us to enjoy the life that God has so graciously given us.

We are motivated by what matters most to us. Paul's method can help us exchange a painful lifestyle for peace. The top-down perspective dictates that we live above these problems, focusing on God's heavenly promises. What could be better than living the good life, beginning now and going on forever? I can't think of two more fulfilling goals!

NOTES

1. Backus and Chapian, *Telling Yourself the Truth*, p. 17 (their emphasis).
2. Ibid., pp. 14-27.